CONTINUOUS IMPROVEMENT MANAGEMENT SYSTEM

Get It Done – Do It Right – Make It Stick

Achieving and Sustaining Operational Excellence

By

Charles Cormier

A practitioner with over 40 years of proven experience

ISBN: 978-1-0688580-0-0

This book is dedicated to my wonderful wife Diane, who has always been loving and supportive as well as being a fantastic mother to our two children.

Table of Contents

AUTHOR'S NOTE **1**

INTRODUCTION **3**

CHAPTER 1: MY JOURNEY **5**

MRPII - *Making it Happen* 7
World Class Manufacturing 10
Just-in-Time: Making it Happen 11
CIMS (Version 1) 13
Take 2 (Boeing Winnipeg) 15
Take 3, CIMS Version 2 (IMP Aerospace) 16
Take 4, CIMS Version 3 (J.D. Irving, Limited) 21
Take 5, CIMS Version 4 (Book) 24

CHAPTER 2: THE FRAMEWORK **27**

Participative Leadership Creates Engagement 31
What Gets Measured, Gets Done 33
A Problem Well Understood, Is Half Solved 34
Chapter Summary / Key Takeaways 36

CHAPTER 3: PLAN MANAGEMENT **37**

Hoshin Kanri 38
Strategic Planning Workshop 40
1. Where do we stand today? 42
2. Where do we want to be? 45
3. What are the barriers? 47
4. How will we overcome the barriers? 50
5. Who must do what? 53
Integrated Business Planning 58
Chapter Summary / Key Takeaways 64

CHAPTER 4: PROJECT MANAGEMENT **67**

Get it Done 69
Do It Right 70
Make It Stick 73
Governance and Structure 76
Project Charter 78
Project Plan 79
Stage Gating Approach 82
Chapter Summary / Key Takeaways 85

CHAPTER 5: PROGRESS MANAGEMENT 87
Make It Visual 88
Progress Meetings 89
Attack the Problem not the Person 91
Five Whys 91
Stop the Line 92
Standardize Work 93
5S+1 Roadmap to the Visual Workplace 94
Virtual Teams 98
Chapter Summary / Key Takeaways 100

CHAPTER 6: PROCESS MANAGEMENT 101
Process Management Standards 103
Model the Business 104
Process Ownership 106
Operating Policies 107
Key Performance Indicators (KPIs) 109
Selecting Processes… to Attack! 112
Improve and Standardize Processes 113
Process Mining 117
Kaizen Blitz 118
Data Governance 122
Chapter Summary / Key Takeaways 125

CHAPTER 7: PERFORMANCE MANAGEMENT 127
Motivation 128
Ability 130
Environment 131
Means & Media 132

Town Hall Meetings 133
Gemba Walks 135
Progress Management 136
Check-Ins 136
Skills Matrix 137
Chapter Summary / Key Takeaways 139

CHAPTER 8: MAKING IT HAPPEN 141
CIMS Maturity Model 144
Takeoff 148
CIMO 151
STOP, … and Think! 153
Chapter Summary / Key Takeaways 156

BIBLIOGRAPHY 157

ACKNOWLEDGMENT 159

ABOUT THE AUTHOR 163

INDEX 165

Author's Note

When I submitted the initial draft of this book to a prospective publisher, they expressed concerns about my references to my experience at Boeing in light of its current situation.

Indeed, my journey in continuous improvement began at Boeing in 1988, a time when the company was at the forefront of innovation and quality, setting industry standards that were the envy of the aerospace world. The emphasis was on creating superior products through meticulous attention to detail, rigorous quality control, and a culture that encouraged continuous improvement.

During my time at Boeing, the company's management systems were designed to ensure every process was optimized for maximum efficiency and quality. Quality and safety were non-negotiable priorities, and there was a strong alignment between operational practices and the company's core values.

Today, however, Boeing faces significant challenges related to quality and safety. Many observers argue that the company's focus has shifted from maintaining high standards to prioritizing profitability.

As someone who hasn't been involved in the aerospace industry for nearly two decades, I must refrain from commenting on Boeing's present situation. However, I trust that readers will evaluate my past experiences at Boeing with objectivity, recognizing the company's historical commitment to quality, safety, and innovation. It's important to note that my professional journey extends beyond aerospace, encompassing various sectors.

Introduction

Most organizations today have adopted improvement programs or applied methodologies such as Lean and Six Sigma and have enjoyed significant improvements. Unfortunately, too many of these organizations see their gains fade very quickly. The improvements do not stick because they are too reliant on the individuals who initially implemented them, and when they move on elsewhere so do their know-how and the discipline that many improvements require to sustain the gains. Moreover, several organizations are only able to achieve localized or pockets of improvements because of a lack of alignment and cohesiveness across the organization. Everyone is on their own so to speak.

World Class companies are generally those who are able to sustain the gains and continuously improve across the whole organization. They have achieved and are able to sustain operational excellence because they have an integrated management system guided by fundamental principles. Toyota is probably the best- and well-known example. The Toyota Production System is their management philosophy and practices to continuously improve the business by identifying and eliminating waste. In essence, it is a Continuous Improvement Management System.

This book presents a framework and integrated approach to truly making continuous improvement a way of life within an organization. There are really no new concepts or improvement methods being suggested here. It is more so about bringing together leading practices to orchestrate continuous improvement across an organization under the three facets of *Get It Done, Do It Right, and Make It Stick.*

The Continuous Improvement Management System (CIMS) presented in this book is the culmination of the author's over 40 years of practical experience across various industries.

CHAPTER 1

My Journey

In 1988, on a Friday morning, there was a yellow sticky-note on my desk... "The General Manager wants to see you ASAP".

At that point, I had been employed two years at Boeing Canada, Arnprior Division as an industrial engineer, working on the implementation and management of their CAD/CAM system (Computer Aided Design & Computer Aided Manufacturing).

Arnprior is a small town, 45 minutes from Ottawa, where the Boeing plant manufactured components and assemblies for the 700 series aircrafts, as well as performed the repair and overhaul of Chinook and Labrador helicopters for the Canadian Government.

The Arnprior division however was going through difficult times. The manufacturing side of the business was not performing well. It had grown a lot and could not keep up with their antiquated planning system, resulting in poor delivery performance and increasing inventory levels. So, the solution was to implement a modern Enterprise Resource Planning (ERP) system, which was referred to in those days as MRPII (MRP 2 – Manufacturing Resource Planning).

The project to implement MRPII started a year or so before that Friday morning when I received the yellow sticky-note. I did not know much about it, just that the project manager's office was next to mine and things were not going so well. I could hear yelling next door and this project manager eventually quit. The project went completely off the rails. A new General Manager was assigned with, let's say, several organizational changes.

It is in this context that I saw the yellow sticky-note. Why would the GM want to see me? Was I part of the restructuring? My wife and I had just purchased our first home.

The new General Manager was Jim Sawyer. He was a long-standing Boeing employee who had grown through the ranks starting as a machinist. His greatest quality, as I came to know him, was his optimism and ability to motivate others in what would seem at times desperate situations.

He had been promoted as General Manager with very clear expectations from Seattle (Boeing's headquarter in those days) that Arnprior needed to be fixed. Its future was at stake.

So, I went to see him on that Friday morning. Until then, I had never really spoken to him.

"You go by Chuck or Charlie?", he said.

"Just Charles, Mr. Sawyer."

"Oh! You can call me Jim. Well as you know Charlie, we are in a tough spot with this MRPII project. I know you know a thing or two about computers so I thought you could take over the project."

"But Mr. Sawyer, Jim I mean, I know nothing about MRPII and I have no project management experience."

"Well, you did a good job implementing CAD/CAM and I am told that you are bright young man. You will figure it out. Anyhow, think about it over the weekend and let's meet again Monday."

I returned to my office dumbfounded. I couldn't stop thinking of how the former project manager next door had been so distressed. But at least, I still had a job.

MRPII - *Making it Happen*

In the office of the former project manager, I found a book titled "MRPII Making it Happen" authored by Thomas F. Wallace and published by Oliver Wight. [1] I couldn't have fallen onto a better book, which I read through the weekend. It explained the '*Proven Path*' to successfully implementing Manufacturing Resource Planning, including the project governance and structure as well as sequence of activities and timeframes.

When I again met Jim Monday morning, I told him I was interested but only if he would read this book. He was a bit taken aback by my request, took the book, slipped through the pages, and reluctantly agreed. The subsequent Monday, we met again.

"Well Charlie, I read the book and I now know why you wanted me to read it. It says that the project leader should be someone seasoned from within the organization. In other words, someone with more experience than you."

"Well yes kind of. But I was thinking…is there someone that I can team up with to lead this project? And also, I need your support that we will follow the *Proven Path*".

"Yes absolutely, this time we got to do it right. I know exactly the guy who can help you make it happen."

The guy was Brian Needham. He too started at Boeing as a machinist, I think almost at the same time as Jim. They were long-time friends. Brian was a no-non-sense straight shooter and very well respected within the organization.

Brian and I really worked well together. I could have not done it without him. In essence, he would take down the 'political' barriers, and I took care of the project management stuff (i.e. Gantt, issues log, etc.).

We secured the services of an Oliver Wight consultant, Paul Hemmen, to help guide us through the *Proven Path*. We chose him because he had aerospace manufacturing experience. He was an older gentleman who came once per month or so for a few days. He was more focused in assuring that we had the proper level of engagement and support from the top. He called it as he saw it, and certainly helped in getting the senior management on board. For instance, when we presented the project plan and budget to the president of Boeing Canada, the president challenged the budget specifically as it related to the amount allocated for training. Paul explained why this level of training was necessary, but the president would not agree. It got a bit heated.

"Too expensive, cut it."

"Please understand that I am here to guide you through a proven path. If you do not want to follow it that is your choice, but in that case, you do not need me."

Paul then stood up, closed his briefcase and walked out of the boardroom. We all looked in dismay. You could see that the president was flustered. A few long seconds later, he went down the hall to catch Paul asking him to return.

The plan and budget were approved, and Paul would remain as our consultant.

I was certainly on a steep learning curve. I learned a lot about how a manufacturing business runs and how to manage an ERP project. The challenge is not really about the technology, but rather having to adopt new business processes.

This project certainly gave me a good appreciation of the challenges in implementing change within an organization. It is not easy when you are trying to change how people have been doing their job for decades. I will always remember what one of the older managers told me.

"Listen young fellow, I was in Bagdad when you were in your dad's bag."

Fortunately, Brian was there to help me navigate through all of this non-sense. The project team eventually gelled, and then things started to happen.

To make a long story short, the project was very successful. It was done on time and within the budget, and it fixed the manufacturing side of the business. The on-time delivery of parts to the assembly lines in Seattle quickly ramped up to the target of 98% and this with a gradual reduction in inventory. Seattle was happy.

In fact, we became the first Boeing division to achieve Class "A" certification. It was actually Tom Wallace (the author of the book "MRPII: Making It Happen) who came and did the audit. We were proud.

I should mention that this did not only happen because we followed the Proven Path but also because we had full support from the top and were blessed with having a topnotch project team.

Through this project I managed to get my APICS (American Production and Inventory Control Society) certification and formal project management training.

World Class Manufacturing

In the meantime, as we were 'fixing' Arnprior, the Boeing Company had bigger concerns then our small division. Airbus was becoming a serious threat to Boeing. Also, the world of manufacturing was changing to Just-in-Time Production, going '*Lean*' the Toyota way. But how could this apply to the aircraft industry where the production rates are much lower than the automotive or electronic industries?

The Boeing senior executives undertook to see how all of these new ways could perhaps apply to our industry. A group of senior executives went on a mission to visit Toyota and other companies in Japan. They were obviously impressed with what they saw and learned, as they returned set and determined to become a world class manufacturer. They recognized however that the change that this would entail to the Boeing way of doing things would be enormous. They realized that it would only happen if everyone understood the burning platform for change. To this end, a video was produced and shown to all Boeing employees in which the President of Airbus was saying in his strong French accent: "We are going to kill the Boeing Company".

Well, that was about the best thing he could have done for Boeing. "*Them's fightin' words.*" as the saying goes.

Boeing engaged expert consultants to help develop and deliver Lean education and training across the whole organization.

Once we learned about Lean at Arnprior, we were primed to get on with it. We had lagged behind in implementing MRPII and this time we wanted to be ahead of the curve. Brian and I were given the mandate to get on with it.

Just-in-Time: Making it Happen

Oliver Wight also had published a book by the above title, authored by Bill Sandras. And lo and behold, we were able to secure his services.

Bill was the kind of consultant that did not tell you exactly what to do but rather helped you think the problem through to the solution. With him nothing was black and white. There were always choices and compromises. He had a lot of experience and wisdom, and I certainly learned a lot from him.

He developed a practical approach to implement Just-in-Time production, which he branded as *One-less-at-a-time* (OLAT). It is based on the recognition that inventory hides problems and that by gradually reducing inventory levels, you can expose and prioritize the next problem that needs to be resolved. This is enabled by converting from a push to a pull production system by using kanbans to control the movement of inventory, and then practicing OLAT by removing kanbans. [2]

A lot of consultants would talk about Lean / JIT in terms of the end-state, such as one-piece flow. But most failed to really explain how to effectively get there. Bill's approach was a '*Proven Path'* to get there.

So, we formed a project team and together we laid out a project plan that would have us implement Lean with a series of one-week Kaizen Blitz (Rapid Improvement Workshops). In essence, we would stop production in an area for one week, and all the employees from this area would participate in reshaping their workplace. A Kaizen Blitz is a participative leadership approach which empowers employees and instills in them a sense of ownership.

In one week, they would accomplish the following:

- Convert from push to pull by implementing kanbans (visual controls) to control inventory.
- Exercise a first cycle of 5S, which is a methodology for organizing the workplace by getting rid of unnecessary things in the workplace and then set and make visible where everything belongs (e.g., floor markings, shadow boards). In essence making sure everything has a place and is in its place.
- Implement a visibility board with key metrics, action list, and cross-training matrix.

And then from that point, each area would practice OLAT and gradually key performance indicators were steadily improving. Lead-times to customer went from months to weeks to days. The results were amazing, and Seattle was taking notice. The Canucks were on to something.

CIMS (Version 1)

While we were implementing Lean, we also learned from the Seattle team that World Class companies had management systems to lead continuous improvement, and that Boeing had adopted a three-part management system consisting of the following:

1. Management by Policy
2. Cross-Functional Management
3. Daily Management

They referred to it as a three-legged stool, implying that it would not stand if one leg was missing.

Management by Policy is the system by which goals are determined, plans to achieve the goals are established, and metrics are implemented to ensure progress towards these goals.

Cross-Functional Management is the system for implementing breakthrough improvements across the organization.

Daily Management is the system used to perform daily activities by establishing reliable methods and consistently pursuing improvements.

Again, we at Arnprior were eager to get on with it. So, Jim asked me to also lead the charge with implementing this management system.

As was the case for Lean, the Boeing Seattle team taught us about the concepts and gave examples but did not really give us an implementation approach. So as Frank Sinatra would say: "I did it my way."

The introduction of the management system became the 'grease' and the 'glue' of continuous improvement. The 'grease' to keep things rolling and the 'glue' to make the improvements stick.

As previously mentioned, Seattle had taken notice of what was happening in Arnprior. Jim eventually got promoted to President of Boeing Canada, and I was promoted as Director of Commercial Programs and Continuous Improvement.

In his new position, Jim reported to the Executive Vice-President of Boeing Commercial Aircraft Group, Bruce Gissing. Mr. Gissing referred to us as Boeing's "test-tube baby". We quickly became recognized as a Lean center of excellence and started to host visits from other Boeing plants. John Black, who was the director of Lean Manufacturing Research and Development for Boeing, came at Arnprior to produce a series of videos. John was the one who pioneered Boeing's Japan study mission and was instrumental in the development of Boeing's World Class Competitiveness course. In a way, he was seeing at Arnprior the fruits of the seeds he had planted. Arnprior emerged as a Lean manufacturing leader within The Boeing Company, earning the Fred Mitchell Award for Lean Manufacturing Excellence three consecutive times, from 2001 to 2003.

(John retired from Boeing in 1999 and started his own consulting firm, working with health care and manufacturing organizations across the world. He also authored a few good books titled "A World Class Production System" [3] and "Lean Production, Implementing a World Class System". [4] He sent me a copy of each book and handwrote in one of them "*To my friend Charles Cormier who started Lean at Boeing*".)

Take 2 (Boeing Winnipeg)

Jim Sawyer, as the new president of Boeing Canada, relocated to Winnipeg, where Boeing had another plant, considerably larger than Arnprior. It is a state-of-the-art facility which manufactures composite parts and assemblies for Boeing Commercial Airplanes. But as far as Lean and management systems were concerned, they were lagging behind, and their performance was less than favorable.

Jim asked if I would be interested in relocating to Winnipeg, but this did not appeal to me for personal reasons. But, of course, I was more than willing to help and guide the Winnipeg team.

We conducted a Kaizen Blitz with the management team, which in essence was to implement a strawman of the management system and set the plan to move forward, including the implementation of Lean.

But both Jim and I were seen as outsiders, so the dynamics were different. It was tough initially, but eventually the Winnipeg team made it happen. It is when they took ownership and 'did it their own way' that it started to really happen. It made me realize that it is not a 'cookie-cutter' approach that will get you there. You need to allow for some latitude and innovation. What really matters are that the principles and concepts are understood and applied. I guess this is why Bill Sandras never really told us exactly what to do. He would more so guide us through a thought process.

In any manner, similarly to Arnprior, they conducted several Kaizen Blitz to implement Lean, and then enjoyed gradual and significant improvements.

Take 3, CIMS Version 2 (IMP Aerospace)

In 1996, I was approached by the IMP Group headquartered in Halifax, Nova Scotia, which is a privately-owned group of companies in diverse sectors such as aerospace & defense, aviation, healthcare, information technology, hospitality, and property development. IMP had an aerospace component manufacturing plant in Amherst, Nova Scotia and they were looking for a general manager.

At this point in our lives, my wife and I had two young kids and saw this as an opportunity to return back east near our families and friends. One side of me regretted leaving a great company and a great job, but I nonetheless decided to make the jump. I had been 10 years with Boeing. Jim was disappointed but he was very supportive. And because I was going to join a Boeing supplier, I was allowed to bring with me a lot of the training material that we had developed over the years.

The understanding I had with IMP is that I would initially assume the role of Director of Operation and transition into the role of General Manager within one year.

Well, let's say that I did not have a full appreciation of what I was walking into. On my first day at work, two Boeing guys who were onsite at IMP came to meet me and stated:

"We are sure glad to see you here. These guys don't get it. We have a hell of a mess on our hands with over 100 AOG's."

AOG stands for "aircraft on ground". It means that the order is a shortage to the aircraft assembly line. At Arnprior it was a crisis if we had more than a handful.

Then an older wiry fellow wearing what seemed to be oversized steel toe boots came to my office.

"So, you're the new guy. I am the Union President, and I just wanted you to know that we don't really like frogs here and I am probably going to become your worst nightmare."

The reference to 'frog' was because I am a French Canadian. He said it with a smirk, so I figured that he was just trying to 'pull my chain'. I calmly replied that it was also my pleasure to meet him.

The Amherst plant was a fallout of a previous company that had gone bankrupt, and employees lost their pension. With government assistance, IMP took over the business and built a new modern plant.

Midweek, I got a visit from a provincial safety officer.

"Listen, we've already issued several orders and you guys are not taking it seriously. Do you realize that you can personally be fined for this?" he stated.

"I am sorry, but I really do not know what you are talking about. I have only joined the company as of this Monday." I replied.

He did not realize I was new to the scene and agreed to give me some slack so I could address the situation.

Every day the two Boeing guys were at my door asking for status on our plan to redress the situation. Normally, under the circumstances, Boeing would pull the tooling and have the work done elsewhere by a more reliable supplier. But the aerospace industry was at capacity, so they were stuck with us at least in the short-term.

There were also several conference calls with other customers such as Bombardier and Bell Helicopter. They too were pretty irate with our poor delivery and quality performance.

My management team was comprised of the managers of quality, production, production control and planning. At our first team meeting on that first week, I asked each of them to brief me on their current situation.

The Production Control Manager stated that we had a lot of shortages and that the customers were very unhappy. I obviously knew that but then asked him what our percentage on-time delivery was.

“I think it is probably around 90%.” he said.

“What do you mean by “I think”? Do you not have a trend chart?” I asked.

“Well, not really. We only measure the number of shortages and with the increase in aircraft build rates plus the onload of new work, it has been getting worst.”

“Ok, could you please look at the last 100 shipments and come back to me with how many were shipped on-time.” I requested.

I then moved on to the quality manager.

"What is our defect rate?"

"It is somewhere arounds 10%, but I too do not really have a metric to show you".

"Well, can you please look at the last 100 orders we completed and tell me the difference between the original order quantity for which we issued material and the final quantity we ended up with".

When we met again on Friday, they both reported their findings. I clearly remember the numbers because coincidently it was the same number of 26%. The on-time delivery was 26% and the defect rate was 26%. These were, to say the least, disastrous numbers.

It was a very long first week. My family was still in Ottawa. We had agreed that I would commute by air once a week for the first three months during which I would relocate my family to the Maritimes.

I arrived home late Friday night. My wife Diane was eagerly awaiting my arrival to hear about my first week at IMP. I walked in, opened the fridge, took a beer, and sat down. She could see that I was somewhat distressed.

"What is wrong Charles?"

"I think I made a big mistake. The place is a total mess. I am thinking of calling Jim to see if I can return to Boeing."

And I went on to explain the situation. She attentively listened and then reminded me why we wanted to return back home.

"I've heard you complain about work before, but you've always found your way through. Is this not the same?" She asked.

Not really, I thought. But what the hell, I might as well give it a go, and worst-case, I will find something else.

I returned on the Monday with determination. I started with the basics by implementing key metrics in the form of trend charts, clearly visible to all employees. As the saying goes: "*What gets measured, gets done*".

We also implemented a basic shop floor priority report and ran daily meetings to monitor progress and deploy action.

I held an all-employee meeting to explain the situation, asking for their help and support. I'd walk the floor at least twice per day to observe and listen.

The AOG count was gradually dropping, and our delivery performance was improving so the Boeing guys were gaining faith, as well as our other customers. But we were still far from being out of the woodworks.

It took a long arduous year to get Operations under control and, as agreed, I was promoted to General Manager, replacing Dave Miller. We had worked well together, and I am sure glad he had been there. He was dealing with the customers, while I was fully focused on fixing the operations or at least bringing it under control. So to speak, he was keeping the wolves at bay, while I was shepherding the herd.

At this point, I had not yet educated my management team on Lean and CIMS, but I was getting ready. We needed some simile of control before we could take a breather and set the proper path forward. During the nights, I would polish my training material. This is when I decided to add Process Management and Performance Management to the framework.

This would become CIMS version 2.

We conducted a first Kaizen Blitz, like the one we held at Boeing Winnipeg, to set the plan forward as well as implement a strawman of CIMS. This led to conducting a series of Kaizen Blitz on the shop floor to implement JIT and 5S, as we had done at Boeing. And again, all performance indicators were showing gradual and steady improvements. Long story short… IMP Aerospace Components became to be recognized as a Supplier of Choice.

Take 4, CIMS Version 3 (J.D. Irving, Limited)

In 2004, I was approached by J.D. Irving (JDI) for the position of Divisional Vice-President.

JDI is a privately-owned conglomerate company headquartered in Saint John, New Brunswick, involved in many industries including forestry, forestry products, agriculture, food processing, transportation, and shipbuilding.

This was a big jump for me and outside of the aerospace industry. I would become vice-president of three companies:

- Kent Homes, a leading manufacturer of modular homes and buildings in Atlantic Canada.

- Universal Truck & Trailer, the largest heavy truck dealership and repair shop in Atlantic Canada.

- Lexitech, the largest translation company in Canada.

This time I did not walk into a dire situation. At the contrary, these three companies were well under control, and JDI already had a well-established Continuous Improvement program in place. The enterprise had fully embraced Six Sigma and had a considerable number of black and green belts. JDI also used Balance Scorecards to set objectives and monitor their progress.

Before having joined JDI, I had read a few books about Six Sigma and Balance scorecards, but I had never applied. So, by working for JDI, I learned and certainly saw the merits of applying these concepts and methods.

But when it came to Lean, JDI was lagging behind. Kent Homes was going to become my 'proof of concept' for JDI. To make a long story short, Kent Homes won the J.K. Irving Outstanding Achievement Award two years in a row.

Jim Irving sent me a nice note stating:

"I would like to once again congratulate you and the Kent Homes team on winning the J.K. Irving Outstanding Achievement Award. It clearly demonstrates the success you have had in leading this team to the next level and creating our internal Center of Excellence for Process Improvement! Your support in exposing the many JDI teams to the 'Power of Unleashing Employee Involvement' has created a

significant move towards a continuous improvement culture. I appreciate the time you have taken personally to be involved in the various presentations and tours in addition to all your other responsibilities in running the business. Charles, your continued support and leadership are greatly appreciated. Our continued focus on 'Finding a Better Way Every Day' will keep us moving and ahead in the race!"

Rheal Maillet, the General Manager of Kent Homes, confessed to me a few years later that he thought that I was coming from the aerospace industry with all these 'sophisticated' ways that would be overkill for a mere home manufacturer. But once it was in place, he conceded that he would never return to the old way.

In 2006, Merv Symes, Vice President of Organizational Change at JDI, became a driving force behind promoting Lean and CIMS across the enterprise. CIMS was eventually branded as "*The Irving Management System*". A few titles of the components were changed but the concepts remained the same. Policy Management became Strategy Management, and Cross-Functional Management became Initiative Management. Also, the balance scorecard was added to the framework as well as other leading practices that JDI had adopted.

In 2009, I was asked to lead a large enterprise program, what is commonly known as an ERP Instance consolidation. JDI wanted to bring all their businesses onto a common ERP platform to achieve economies of scale and standardize best practices across the organization. It was, in essence, an enterprise-wide business process improvement initiative.

The program was named Enterprise One (E1) with the tag line "*All for One, and One for All.*"

After one year into E1, I was also asked to take over the I.T. Division's Project Management Office (PMO), which had the mandate to provide governance and oversight of IT projects across the enterprise. There was a lot on the go. However, the PMO was really only in its infancy. They had recently implemented a new Portfolio and Project Management system, but the processes were not standardized, nor was there any metrics to monitor the projects. So, this is where we started by defining and implementing metrics, and then standardizing the project management approach. We were really applying Process Management on Project Management.

I ran the PMO for over a decade and suffice it to say that I learned a lot, which would help me bring further improvements to CIMS, especially in the area of project management of course.

Additionally, working for nearly two decades with a conglomerate involved in numerous industries allowed me to gain valuable experience and validate my belief that the fundamentals of continuous improvement are universally applicable.

Take 5, CIMS Version 4 (Book)

Over the years, it was suggested on a few occasions that I write a book about CIMS, given my passion for it and its proven effectiveness. As I approach the end of my professional journey, I decided to take on this challenge. In doing so, I refreshed the model to make it more comprehensive and intuitive.

This book presents a framework illustrating how leading practices can be harmonized to make continuous improvement a fundamental aspect of an organization's operations. While it doesn't delve deeply into each practice and methodology, it provides sufficient explanation for readers to understand their application and significance within the CIMS framework.

Get it done, do it right and make it stick!

CHAPTER 2

The Framework

A framework, as a structured management system, is implemented to supplant informal management practices, which typically exhibit the following symptoms:

a) A lot of things fall through the cracks.

b) Always seem to be in crisis mode… firefighting.

c) Blame culture… attack the person not the problem.

d) Decision making often based on gut feeling, not with facts and data.

e) Problem solving based on symptoms, not root causes.

f) A lot of "Management by Excuse".

g) Everyone not pulling in the same direction.

h) Confusion and frustration.

i) Etc.

In essence, the informal management system can be epitomized as '*managing by the seat of your pants*'.

World Class management systems have the following characteristics:

a) Modeled on the *'Plan-Do-Check-Act'* wheel.

b) Focused on continuous improvement.

c) Built on people involvement.

d) Use facts and data for decision making.

e) Get to the root cause for problem solving.

f) Guided by fundamental principles.

My first exposure to a World Class Management System was referred to as a "three-legged stool" comprised of Policy Management, Cross-Functional Management and Daily Management, as illustrated in Figure 2.1.

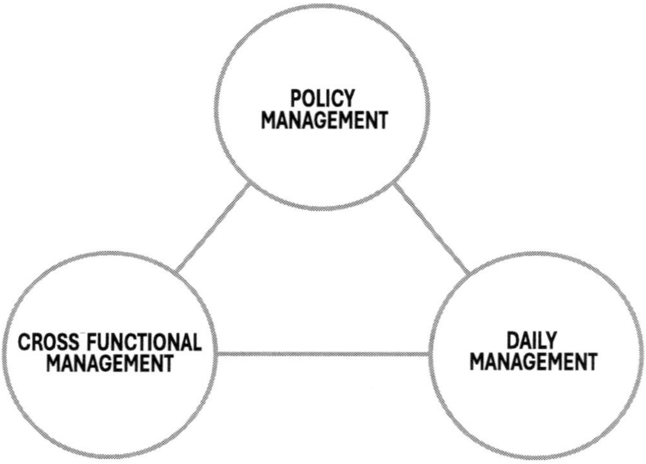

Figure 2.1 – World Class Management System adopted by Boeing in the 1990's

Policy Management is about setting strategies and deploying goals supported by initiatives. Cross-functional Management is about implementing these initiatives and achieving step-change improvements. Daily Management is about executing the work and incrementally improving.

I learned that World Class companies apply a continuous cycle of standardizing, stabilizing, and improving their business processes, as well as assure the continuous growth and learning of their employees. When you think about it, it really talks to Process Management and Performance Management. So, I thought that these should be called out separately and added to the framework.

Then when I better understood Cross-Functional and Daily Management, I thought that the titles did not best describe their purpose. In essence, Cross-functional Management is what would commonly be known as Project Management. And Daily Management is about moving forward, not losing the gains. In other words, it about managing progress. I always get a kick when people say that they are having their weekly Daily Management meeting. So, I thought that calling it "Progress Management" better captures the intent.

As for Policy Management, I do not really fancy the term "policy" in this context, as it sounds too much like rules. Instead, I believe "Plan Management" better describe its purpose.

Now having 5P's is kind of cool. It resonates well with the 5S's of workplace organization and the 5 Why's of problem solving. So, 5 P's it is.

Figure 2.2 illustrates the framework of my version 4 of the Continuous Improvement Management System (CIMS). Each of the sub-systems is described briefly below and will be covered in more detail in the chapters that follow.

Figure 2.2 - Continuous Improvement Management System

Plan Management is at the top because it sets direction to the "True North", which is a key concept of process improvement. It is an idiom that emerged from Toyota, connotes the compass needle for Lean transformation. True North works as a compass to take an organization from the current condition to where they want to be. That is what Plan Management is all about. It is used to identify strategic initiatives which feeds into Project Management, which in turn drives the execution of these initiatives. Plan Management also establishes the organization's goals and maintains an integrated business plan, which feeds into Progress Management.

Both Project and Progress Management draw on and feed into Process Management by which processes are standardized and optimized. Process improvement projects will often result in significant changes to processes. Progress Management drives standardization of work to capture and maintain best practices which will continuously evolve. Process Management includes the framework and approach to manage the business processes.

Then in the center of the CIMS framework, with the circle purposely larger, is Performance Management, which motivates employees' growth and development aligned to the organization's goals. It is the heart of CIMS because it is the employees who truly make it happen.

CIMS is an integrated approach to achieving *Continuous Improvement as a Way of Life*, which is guided by three fundamental and interrelated principles:

1. Participative Leadership Creates Engagement.
2. What Gets Measured, Gets Done.
3. A Problem Well Understood is Half Solved.

It is important to note that these principles are not mutually exclusive. They are like a three-legged stool, ...if one leg is missing, then the stool will not stand.

Participative Leadership Creates Engagement

Simply put, employee who are not in the know and who do not feel part of it, cannot be expected to be highly engaged.

In the proper setting, having employees involved in making decisions and implementing them can greatly increase their engagement. It really falls on the leaders of the organization to foster a culture of trust and openness to allow for true participative leadership.

In the context of CIMS, participative leadership is not just about involving employees, but it is also about leaders themselves being significantly visible and involved. The leaders must help remove barriers as well as coach and guide the team. Sometimes the leaders must roll their sleeves and get their hands dirty.

Strategic planning will not be limited to senior executives. It will also include key players from the different levels of the organization. Goals will be set by applying a technique known as "Catchball", by which consensus is achieved.

Project Plans will be built with the participation of the team members. In other words, they will not be brought into a project to execute an already baked plan. Building the plan together will create greater ownership and accountability.

Regular team meetings will be held to review progress and identify opportunities for improvements to then be actioned by the team.

Senior Management will be visible and conduct regular process checks to help identify opportunities. These are referred to as "Gemba Walks". The term "gemba" comes from Japanese and it means "the real place". In Lean management, "Gemba" is the most important place for a team as it is the place where the real work happens.

Kaizen Blitz will be conducted to 'attack' problems and improve processes.

This all being said, it is important to understand that Participative leadership does not mean that the leaders give the reins away. Ultimately, they still are accountable for decisions taken that fall under their responsibilities. But in the spirit of trust and openness, the leaders must always explain why if they do not agree with the team.

What Gets Measured, Gets Done

Or another way of saying it: "What doesn't get measured, doesn't get managed".

CIMS will establish and deploy goals, which are SMART, meaning that they are specific, measurable, actionable, realistic, and timely. The corresponding measures will be presented in the form of trend charts to monitor progress against the targets. These will clearly be visible in the workplace, so employees can see at a glance if they are gaining or losing ground. Or another way of saying it, the team knows if they are "winning or losing the game".

Processes will be defined and measured in terms of their effectiveness and efficiency. Just by measuring them exposes opportunities for improvements. Furthermore, benchmarking against industry leading practices can further expose opportunities.

Tasks and action items will be documented with clear due dates, against which progress will be monitored. This too will be visible in the workplace in the form of an opportunity board or sheet.

(It has been my experience that just by implementing metrics and making them visible to the team, things will happen. For instance, when I joined IMP, we implemented a visibility board in the cafeteria with trend charts for quality, cost, delivery, and safety. None had targets on the charts at that point. We also included pareto charts to highlight opportunities by area. Within a few months, trends were showing improvements. The most noticeable one was productivity which improved by 7% without implementing any real improvement at that point. It was simply the competitive spirit that kicked in.)

A Problem Well Understood, Is Half Solved

This principle is a slight variation to the saying "A problem well-stated is half-solved", which was said by Charles Kettering, the famed inventor, and head of research for General Motors. It is really about bringing clarity to the real problem. On one hand it is about clearly articulating the problem (i.e., well stated), and to go further, it is truly getting to the root cause of the problem (i.e., well understood).

For example, you may say that the problem you have is that you need a new batterie for your car. But you are really suggesting a solution and not clearly articulating the problem. The real problem is that your battery is dead, and you cannot start the car. But when you get to the root cause, you may realize that the alternator is not working because the belt is broken and well beyond its life expectancy. So now the solution is becoming obvious. (I am using this example, because I learned this lesson with my first car, an old rust-bucket I had as a student.)

Albert Einstein is reported to have said that if he only had one hour to solve a problem, he would spend 55 minutes defining the problem and the remaining 5 minutes solving it routinely.

CIMS will therefore want to have clear problem statements and get to the root cause. Strategies, which are solutions, will be established only once the problems are well understood. Problems will not be stated with implied solutions. We will apply the Toyota "5 Why" technique, which is an iterative interrogative technique used to explore the cause-and-effect relationships underlying a particular problem.

In all of this, we will attack the problem and not the person.

Chapter Summary / Key Takeaways

CIMS is an integrated approach to achieving *Continuous Improvement as a Way of Life.* It is comprised of the following 5 sub-systems:

- Plan Management to establish the *'True North'* and set the plan to navigate the organization towards it.
- Project Management to implement the strategic initiatives and achieve step-change improvements.
- Progress Management to incrementally improve performance.
- Process Management to standardize and optimize business processes.
- Performance Management to motivate employees' growth and development aligned to the goals of the organization.

CIMS is guided by three fundamental and interrelated principles:

1. Participative Leadership Creates Engagement.
2. What Gets Measured, Gets Done.
3. A Problem Well Understood is Half Solved.

CHAPTER 3

Plan Management

Plan Management involves the ongoing process of creating, implementing, monitoring, and adjusting a business plan to ensure that an organization successfully achieves its goals.

It starts with setting strategic goals and initiatives.

Strategies set direction and an overarching approach that the organization will take to achieve its goals. The strategies are brought to action mainly through strategic initiatives coupled with more granular objectives deployed throughout the organization to ensure alignment.

Hoshin Kanri

Hoshin Kanri, also known as Policy Deployment or Hoshin Planning, is a strategic planning method used to align an organization's functions and activities with its strategic goals. The term "Hoshin" means "compass" or "direction" in Japanese, and "Kanri" means "management" or "control." Together, Hoshin Kanri translates to "direction management" or "management by direction."

Some will say that it is Management by Objective (MBO) done the right way. A major deficiency of the traditional MBO is that as goals are deployed, the means to achieve the goals do not necessarily exist. Hoshin Kanri extends the MBO process and uses a bottom-up approach to determine the method of achievement. It is heavily oriented towards the process of achieving the goals, so that true progress is made by improving the business rather than just working harder and taking advantage of fortuitous windfall gains.

The following summarizes the differences between the traditional MBO and Hoshin Kanri:

MBO	Hoshin Kanri
Focus on results	Focus on process to get results
Top Down	Top Down / Bottom Up
"Strong Arm" Tactic	Goals & actions negotiated
Focus on Who	Focus on How
Individualistic	Group Oriented
Work Harder	Work Smarter
Who Failed?	What went wrong?
Can demoralize	Can energize

Key elements of Hoshin Kanri include:

1. Vision and Mission: Clearly defining the organization's long-term vision and mission is the foundation. This involves understanding the core purpose of the organization and where it aims to be in the future.
2. Strategic Objectives: Establishing 3- to 5-year breakthrough objectives aligned with the vision and mission. These objectives should be specific, measurable, achievable, relevant, and time-bound (SMART).
3. Annual Objectives: Breaking down the long-term objectives into annual goals. These goals should be achievable within a year and directly contribute to the breakthrough objectives.
4. Deployment: Cascading the annual objectives down through the organization. This involves translating the high-level goals into specific actions and targets for departments, teams, and individuals.
5. Catchball Process: A back-and-forth communication process where goals and plans are discussed, negotiated, and refined between different levels of the organization. This ensures that objectives are realistic and that there is buy-in at all levels.
6. Implementation: Executing the plans at every level of the organization. This requires detailed action plans, timelines, resource allocation, and regular monitoring.
7. Review and Adjust: Regularly reviewing progress towards the goals. This involves checking if the objectives are being met and making necessary

adjustments to the plans or strategies. It ensures continuous improvement and responsiveness to changing circumstances.

Strategic Planning Workshop

The process normally starts by conducting a strategic planning workshop that includes senior management and other key stakeholders from various parts of the organization. This workshop should address the following five fundamental questions:

1. Where do we stand today?
2. Where do we want to be?
3. What are the barriers?
4. How will we overcome them?
5. Who must do what?

In doing so, we will want to apply a system thinking approach by:

- Capturing everyone's concerns (issues) and thoughts (opinions)
- Rationalizing the inter-relationships of these concerns and thoughts

The workshop normally takes three to five days. Ideally, it should be held offsite so to minimize interruptions.

Setting a strategic plan and achieving consensus can be challenging for the following reasons:

a) There may a be a lot of issues to consider, making it difficult to rationalize.

b) There may be one overwhelming issue which clouds all other important issues.

c) People will come with preconceived views and opinions.

d) The more vocal may take over the meeting.

e) Some may not dare to argue with the boss.

f) Some will not voice their opinions (fence sitters).

g) Some will have different thinking patterns.

I will therefore offer an approach to navigate through these 'rough waters' that I learned many years ago and have successfully applied on numerous occasions. My first introduction to this approach was at Boeing. It was actually my very first time involved in a strategic planning session. I remember sitting in the cafeteria with the directors of operations and human resources who both were saying that our biggest problem was poor employee morale. They had previously been involved in strategic planning sessions but this time a consultant was engaged to walk us through a new approach. The consultant came from California, a rather flamboyant fellow, wearing a suit with sneakers, which in those days was a bit unusual. He nonetheless did a great job facilitating the session and in walking us through an interesting approach. It made the leadership team realize that employee morale was actually an outcome and not a driver. More impressively, it brought the whole leadership team to a consensus on the strategic goals and initiatives.

That, in itself, was a breakthrough according to the 'old-timers'.

Firstly, it requires an experienced and neutral facilitator to guide the group through the approach and to apply the various facilitating techniques to promote participation, keep the group focused, and all that jazz.

Here are the rules of engagement for the workshop:

1. Be prepared… do your homework.
2. Be punctual and present… unplug your devices.
3. Be open and respectful… listen, do not interrupt.
4. Be engaged… argue your points… Silence is Approval.
5. Be candid… attack the problem, not the person.
6. Be compromising to seek consensus.

As for the first point, the only real preparedness required by some of the participants relates to answering the first question.

1. Where do we stand today?

There are two aspects to this question. One is in terms of the organization's stance and the other in terms of its performance.

The organization's stance is normally articulated in a mission statement and a declaration of its core values. The organization's mission is its purpose of being. And core values are what the organization stands for. These are important because they help in the decision-making process and motivate the proper behaviors. They can also help build customer and public confidence. Moreover, they can have a significant influence on recruitment and retention of employees.

If the mission and core values are already documented, then it is good to simply review and validate that they still hold true, or simply to reassert them. If they are not documented, then this is a good opportunity to have the group build a strawman. Then someone can be tasked to wordsmith proper statements.

As for the organization's performance, we want to review where we stand relative to four perspectives, which was reinforced by the so-called Balance Scorecard (BSC), originally developed by Dr. Robert Kaplan of Harvard University and Dr. David Norton as a framework for measuring organizational performance. [5] The four perspectives include:

1. Financial: this perspective views organizational financial performance and the use of financial resources.

2. Customer/Stakeholder: this perspective views organizational performance from the point of view of the customer or other key stakeholders that the organization is designed to serve.

3. Internal Process: this perspective views organizational performance through the lenses of the quality and efficiency related to the product, services, and key business processes.

4. Organizational Capacity (or Learning and Growth): views organizational performance through the lenses of human capital, infrastructure, technology, culture, and other capacities that are key to breakthrough performance.

Therefore, we want to understand where the organization currently stands by reviewing key performance indicators (KPIs) for each of these perspectives. Understanding where we stand today needs to be brought into perspective with respect to our progress over time and therefore KPIs should be presented in the form of trend charts. Moreover, we need to understand where we stand to expectations and as compared to industry trends and best practices.

Other forms of presenting the data can be used to help give greater insights and bring to light the most fruitful opportunities. This may be in the form of pareto charts, pie charts, heat maps, etc.

After having reviewed all this information, the team summarizes the key findings in the form of a SWOT, which stands for Strengths, Weaknesses, Opportunities, and Threats. Strengths and weaknesses are internal to your organization —things that you have some control over and can change. Opportunities and threats are external things that are going on outside your organization. You can take advantage of opportunities and protect against threats, but you can't change them.

At this point, we have our bearings, i.e., we know where we stand.

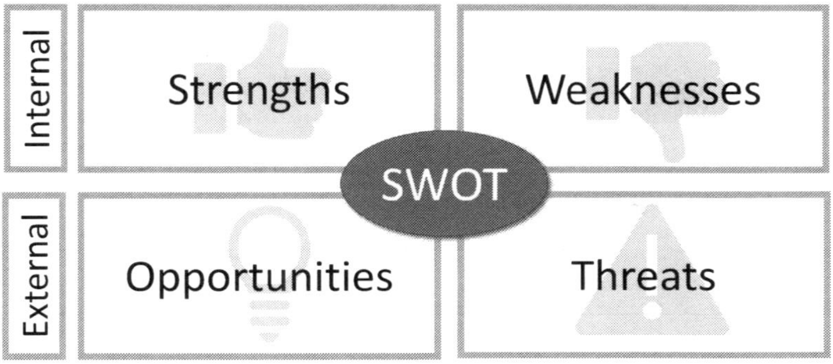

Figure 3.1 – SWOT Analysis

2. Where do we want to be?

This question is answered by articulating a vision statement and setting strategic goals.

A vision statement defines what we want to be like in the future, thus giving a sense of purpose, inspiring the development and growth of the organization. It is an image of the future one seeks to create. It helps steer the strategies by repeatedly asking the question: 'How does this help us achieve our vision?' It also gives direction for employee behavior and inspires them to bigger and better things.

If a Vision Statement is already documented, then it is good to simply review and validate that it still holds true, as well to validate that it is clear, concise, and inspirational.

If one has not yet been articulated, then the team should build a strawman. And again, someone can be tasked to wordsmith a statement.

We now can move on in defining strategic goals towards achieving the Vision statement. These goals normally go out 3 to 5 years, but do not necessarily result in achieving the

Vision but rather brings the organization on the right path towards it as illustrated in Figure 3.2. As previously stated, goals must be 'SMART', meaning that they are specific, measurable, actionable, realistic, and timely.

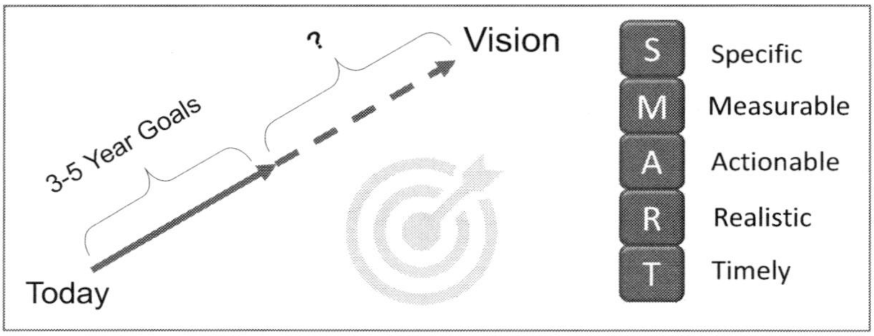

Figure 3.2 - Setting Goals towards achieving the Vision

Ideally, strategic objective should be set within the framework of the balance scorecard as illustrated in Figure 3.3.

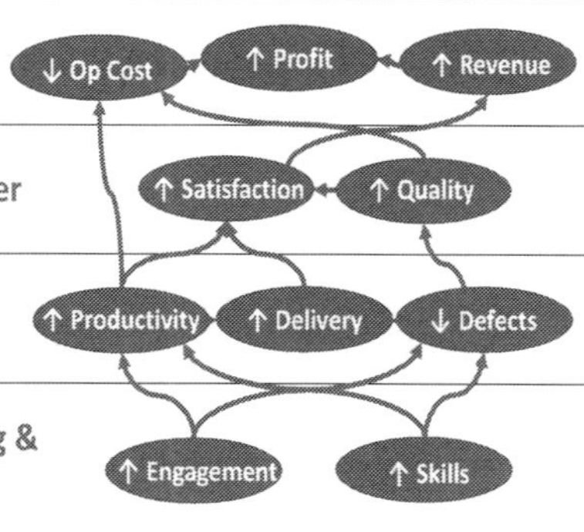

Goals Strategy Map	Measure	Target
Finance	Revenue Net Profit Op Cost	
Customer	Net Promoter Warranty Claims	
Internal Process	On-time Delivery Defect Rate Labour Variance	
Learning & Growth	EE Dev Plans Attrition	

Figure 3.3 - Goal Strategy Map

3. What are the barriers?

On the basis that a *problem well understood is half solved*, we need to understand what are the barriers that we need to overcome in order to achieve the goals. We then can set and prioritize the solutions to remove or circumvent these barriers.

Identifying the barriers involves three steps, which are illustrated in Figure 3.4 and further explained as follows.

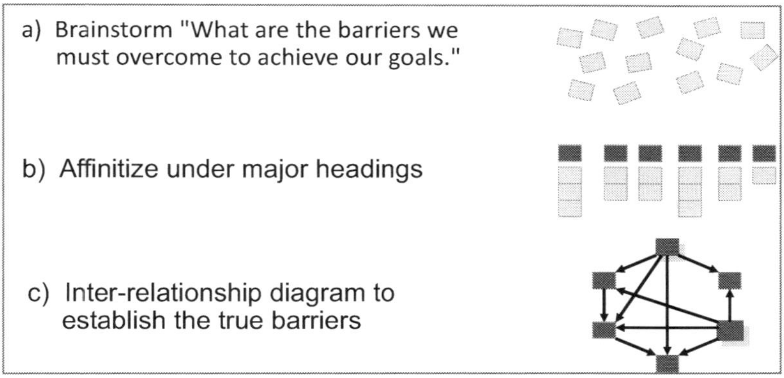

Figure 3.4 - Steps to identifying the true barriers.

a) Brainstorm: Capture everyone's opinions of what they believe are the barriers. Barriers can be conditions, perceptions, attitudes, constraints, problems, or anything else that need to be either eliminated, mitigated, reduced, resolved, or circumvented in order to achieve the goals. These barriers are scribed on yellow sticky-notes and randomly posted on the wall.

   It is important that all opinions be captured and not challenged or criticized at this stage. Before starting, participants should be reminded that all ideas are welcome, and no judgments will be made during the initial idea generation phase. This helps in uncovering genuine concerns and potential barriers. Also, a 'going around the table' approach should be used during the brainstorming session to ensure everyone has an opportunity to contribute.

b) Affinitize: Group barriers in columns where there seems to be an affinity between them and assign a title to each group that describes the general theme. Here is a simple example of three groups with the titles in bold:

Poor Data Quality	**Poor Cust. Experience**	**Unreliable Processes**
Can't rely of data	Cumbersome ordering	Process variation
Dirty data	Customer complaints	No proper standards
Data entry errors	Slow to respond	Tribal knowledge
No data ownership	Lack of follow-through	Inconsistent methods
Missing data	Unfulfilled promises	Outdated procedures
Duplicate info	Poor customer service	Incapable processes
	Long customer waits	

Going through this exercise can easily result in 20 columns or so.

Affinitizing is performed as follows:

i. Sort Silently: The participants go to the wall and independently sort the ideas into groups and in silence to avoid influencing each other's thinking. There's no need to label the groups at this stage; focus on grouping similar items together.

ii. Discuss and Refine Groups: Once initial groups are formed, the facilitator reviews and discusses with the team the reasoning behind each grouping. This normally results in merging, splitting, or rearranging groups as needed based on the team's consensus.

iii. Label the Groups: After refining the groups, the facilitator with the team's input assigns a title to each group that describes the general theme or relationship among the ideas in that group.

c) Rationalize: Finally, we want to identify the true barriers that we need to contend with. To do so, the titles of each group need to be duplicated and then posted in a big circle on brown paper or on a whiteboard. Then we go around the circle establishing the interdependencies between each and every one. A line is drawn from the cause with the arrow pointing to the effect. So, using my example, the facilitator would ask the group: "Does poor data quality cause unreliable processes, or does unreliable processes cause poor data quality, or is there no link between both?". The group would most likely say that unreliable processes cause poor data quality and so a line would be drawn between both with the arrow pointing to poor data quality.

Once through the whole circle, it will look like a spiderweb as shown in Figure 3.5. No worries. What really matters is the number of lines and arrows toughing each barrier. Barriers that mostly have arrows pointing to them, means that they are more so outcomes or symptoms of the true barriers.

Inversely, barriers that have most of the lines without arrows means that they are causes, hence the true barriers. Normally this exercise will reveal a handful of true barriers.

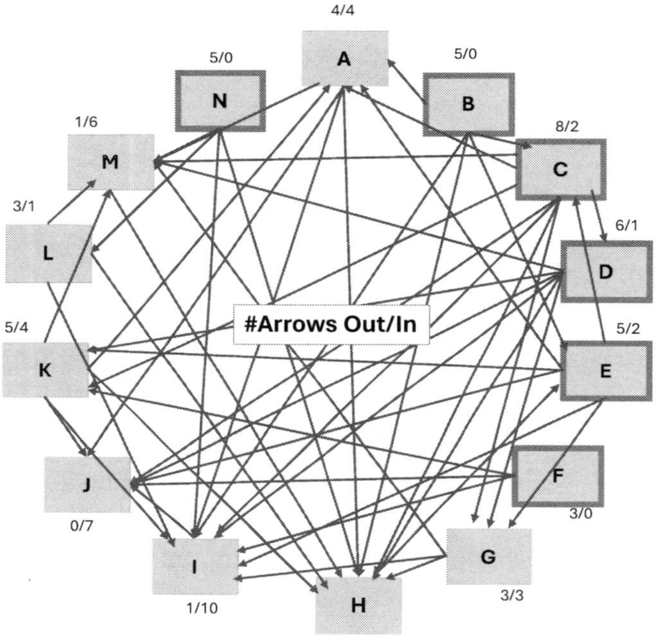

Figure 3.5 – Identifying the true barriers through cause-and-effect analysis.

4. How will we overcome the barriers?

At this point, the team has a good understanding of what they need to contend with and can explore potential solutions. Solutions encompasses any decisions, directions or actions that can be taken to overcome the true barriers. They may transpire either into policies, strategies, initiatives, projects or 'just-do-it'.

Again, we are going to do this in three steps as illustrated in Figure 3.6.

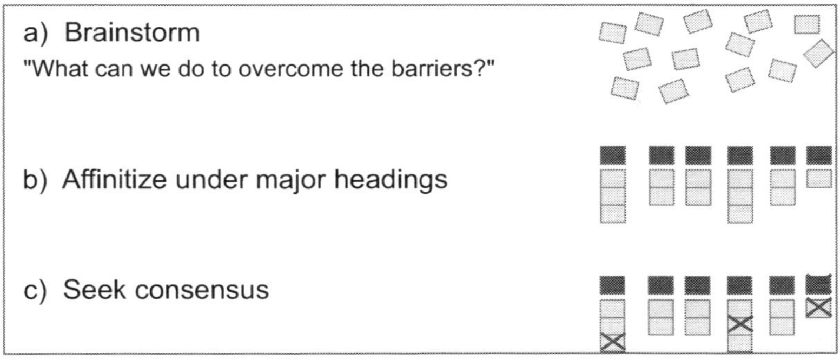

Figure 3.6 – Identifying Solutions

The first two steps are the same as before except instead of barriers, we are exploring solutions. The third step, however, differs in that we seek consensus on the proposed solutions for each group as a whole and on the ideas within the group. Take as an example the following two groups of ideas:

Modernize ERP
Upgrade ERP system
~~Replace ERP solution~~
Improve IT platform
Leverage ERP functionality
Go to the Cloud
Enable mobile
Improve data warehouse

~~**Grow through acquisitions**~~
~~Acquire ABC company~~
~~Partner with XYZ~~
~~Part ownership of ZZZ~~
~~Buy smaller competitor~~

The team agreed with having to modernize their ERP system, but not replace it. And with respect to the second group, the team decided that it would not proceed with the idea to grow by acquisition. Perhaps because they simply do not have the funds to make it happen.

At this stage, we have many good ideas, but attempting to tackle them all at once would probably not bear fruit. In fact, one of the lessons learned from many organizations is that when it comes to breakthrough improvements, it is best to focus on the few that have the greatest impact.

Therefore, we want to conduct an impact analysis as illustrated in Figure 3.7. It simply involves rating the impact that each solution would have on each true barrier. Then the solutions can be prioritized based on their overall level of impact.

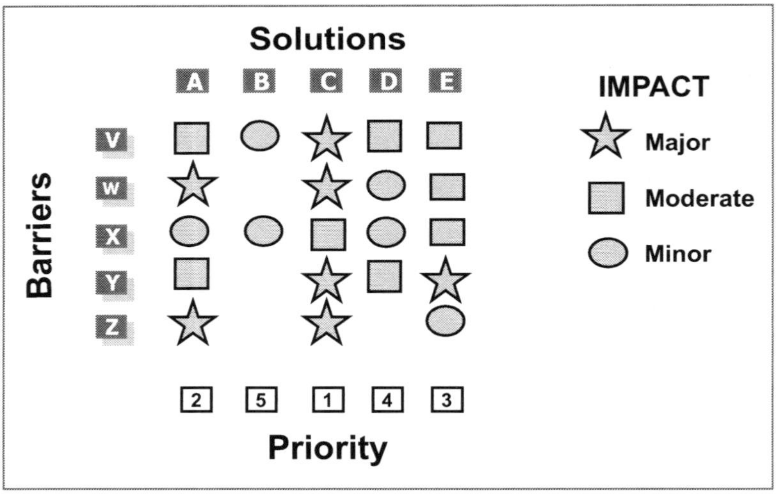

Figure 3.7 – Prioritization of Solutions

In doing this analysis, you may choose to give a weight to each of the barriers to reflect their level of importance to the success of the organization. For instance, you could apply 3,2 and 1 for high, medium, and low respectively for both the importance of the barriers and the impact of the solutions. Then the solution with the greatest sum of the multiplications of these two factors would be considered the highest priority.

It is up to this point in the strategic planning process that the consultant from California carried us. I have since applied this approach on many occasions and, in all instances, consensus was achieved. I even had a strategic planning session where the union executives were invited to participate. This is when I was at IMP, where we really needed their input and buy-in on fixing the business. They initially came in with their arms crossed, but once we got into it, they became engaged and helped us build our strategic plan. This was a turning point in our working relationship.

5. Who must do what?

Hoshin Planning is like a management compass that points everyone in the organization in the same direction towards a common destination. Some will say that it weaves the "Golden Thread", by which everyone can see how their team's objectives link to the strategic goals of the organization.

The approach involves cascading goals and objectives as well as establishing the means to achieve them and it is normally conducted as part of an annual planning cycles. It involves an iterative process of negotiating objectives, known as "Catchball" by which expectations and ideas are thrown back and forth between managers and their team until they can establish reasonable objectives supported by action plans to achieve them.

An effective tool to cascade goals and objectives is the X-matrix as shown in Figure 3.8.

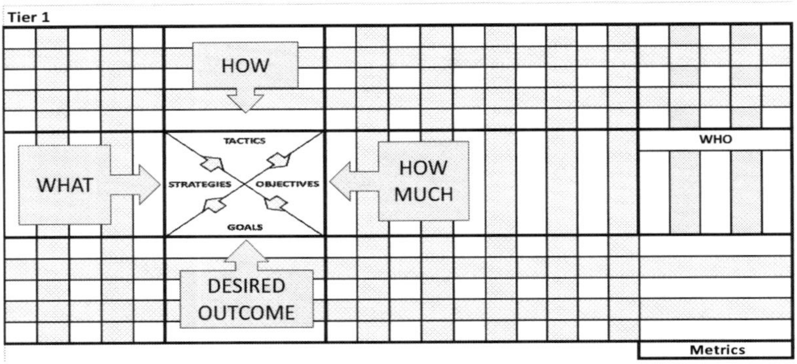

Figure 3.8 - X-Matrix

The x-matrix is filled clockwise starting with the "Desired Outcomes", and then establishing "What" will be done, "How" it will be done, by "How much" and by "Who".

The process starts by defining the tier 1 x-matrix, which then is cascaded to tier 2 x-matrices, and if required to a tier 3 level.

A simple example of a tier 1 x-matrix is shown in Figure 3.9. Then Figure 3.10 shows how the tier 1 is cascaded to a tier 2. The corresponding tier 2 x-matrix is shown in Figure 3.11.

At this juncture, the goals, objectives, strategies, and tactics are clearly defined. This will now feed into the other components of CIMS to make it happen.

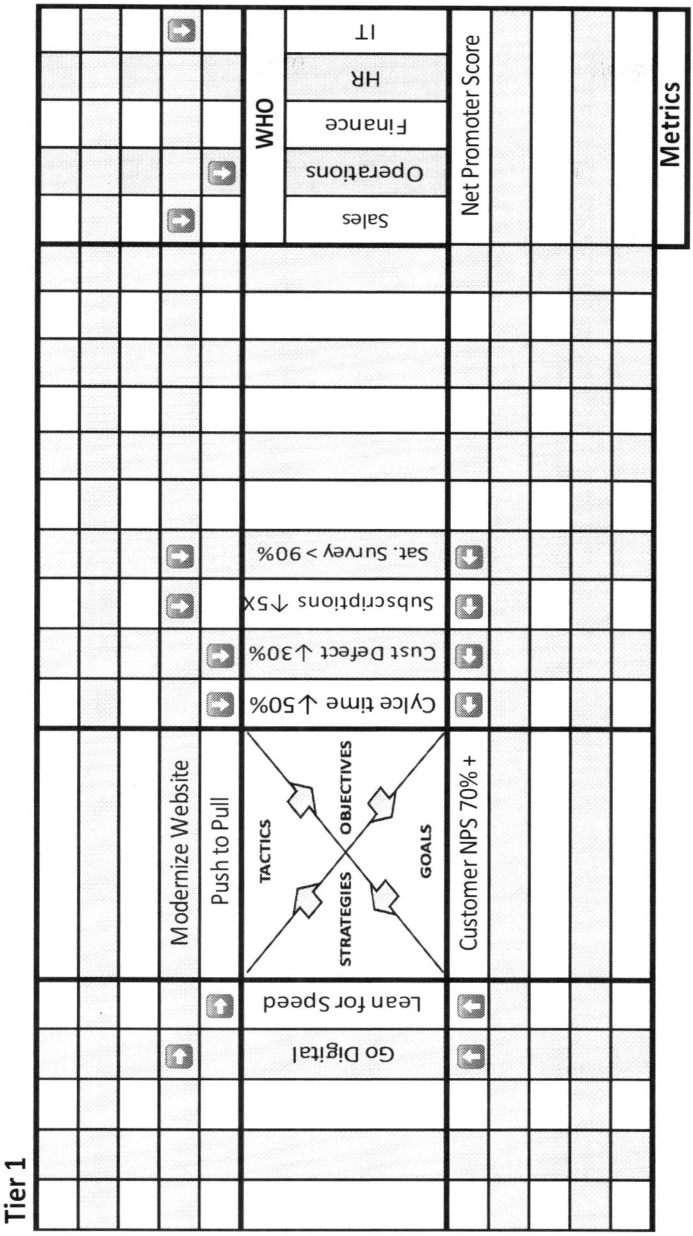

Figure 3.9 – Example of tier 1 X-Matrix

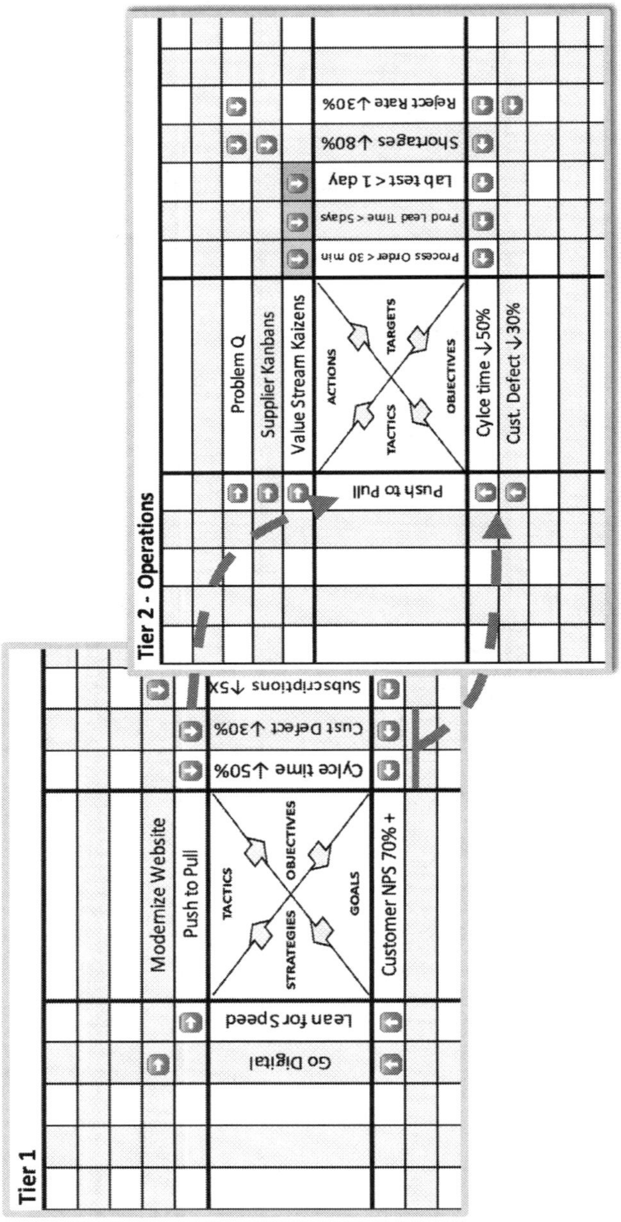

Figure 3.10 – Cascade of tier 1 to tier 2 x-matrix

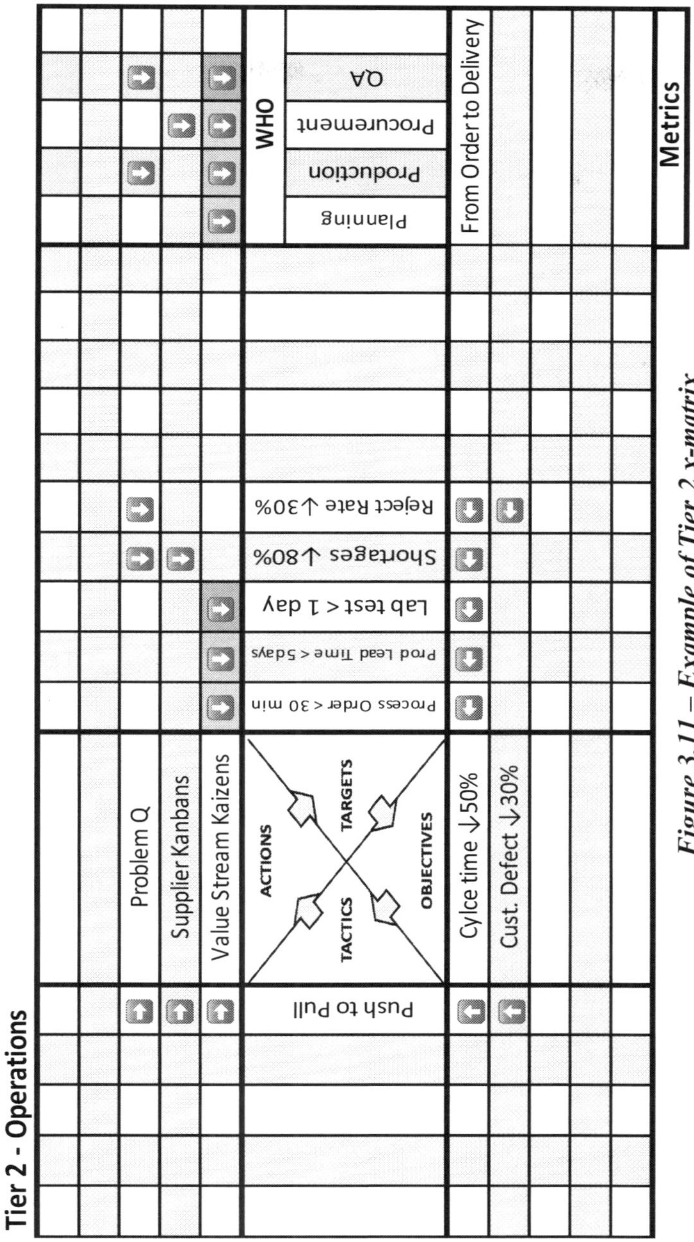

Figure 3.11 – Example of Tier 2 x-matrix

Integrated Business Planning

Integrated Business Planning (IBP), originally referred to as Sales and Operation Planning, is a strategic management process that aligns the various functions within the organization to a unified plan that balances supply and demand. It is crucial for operationalizing an organization towards achieving its strategic goals because it ensures alignment, coherence, and effective execution across all levels and functions of the organization.

IBP involves forecasting the customer demand on the organization and aligning the resources to optimally satisfy the demand to the extent possible. It focuses on the operational aspects of the organization, mid- to long-term planning and decision-making typically covering a horizon of several months out to as long it is required to plan and commit resources.

The difference between supply and demand results in either lost opportunities, over-production, or underutilization of resources. Over-production results in inventory. Where inventory resides, relative to supply and demand, depends on the business operating model to satisfy demand, which is normally one of the following:

- Production is only executed on demand, referred in to as build-to-order.
- Production is executed ahead of anticipated demand, referred as build-to-stock.
- A blend of both resulting in having semi-finished goods on hand.

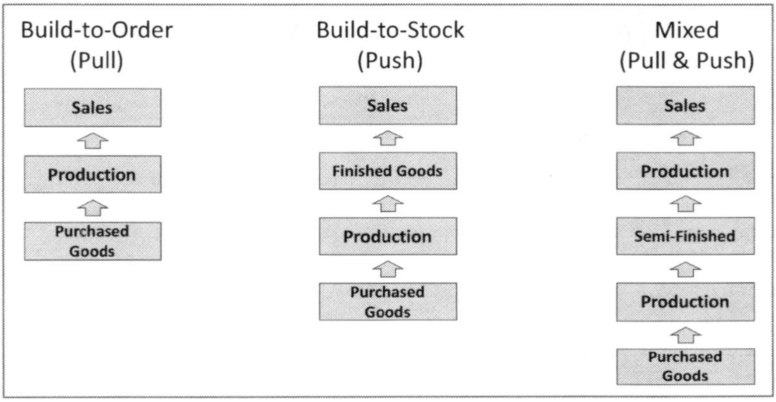

Figure 3.12 – Business Operating Models to Satisfy Demand

The integrated business plan should therefore be laid out to reflect the applicable business model.

IBP involves planning all the inputs and outputs of the business processes involved in satisfying customer demands while aiming to achieve organizational goals. In essence it is the balancing of supply and demand throughout the supply chain of the organization. These inputs and outputs include products, services, funds, and resources.

The plan should reflect the anticipated improvements from strategic initiatives, such as reducing cycle time, increasing yield, and boosting productivity.

The plan is best represented in a time-phased view, normally in monthly buckets, of the key variables that come in to play in satisfying customer demand. An example of an integrated business plan is shown in Figure 3.13. You will note that in this example the plan is aiming to improve productivity, reduce inventory, increase sales and improve margins.

		Jan	Feb	Mar	Apr	May	Jun	Jul	Aug	Sep	Oct	Nov	Dec	Jan2	Feb2	Mar2
Cash from Ops	Plan	160	168	206	216	254	242	368	357	367	312	270	365	247	236	224
($000)	Actual	161	(16)	241												
	Variance	1	(184)	35												
Margin	Plan	15.0%	15.1%	15.2%	15.2%	15.3%	15.4%	15.5%	15.5%	15.6%	15.7%	15.8%	15.8%	15.9%	16.0%	16.1%
(%)	Actual	14.0%	13.9%	14.1%												
	Variance	-1.0%	-1.2%	-1.1%												
Sales	Plan	1,200	1,200	1,250	1,250	1,300	1,300	1,350	1,350	1,400	1,400	1,400	1,400	1,400	1,400	1,400
($000)	Actual	1,100	1,000	1,300												
	Variance	(100)	(200)	50												
Inventory	Plan	3,000	3,015	2,995	2,965	2,900	2,850	2,662	2,487	2,311	2,202	2,143	1,972	1,943	1,929	1,930
($000)	Actual	2,500	2,680	2,612												
	Variance	(500)	(335)	(383)												
Production	Plan	1,200	1,215	1,230	1,220	1,235	1,250	1,162	1,175	1,224	1,291	1,341	1,229	1,371	1,386	1,401
($000)	Actual	1,201	1,180	1,232												
	Variance	1	(35)	2												
Productivity	Plan	0.80	0.81	0.82	0.83	0.84	0.85	0.86	0.87	0.88	0.89	0.90	0.91	0.92	0.93	0.94
(Index)	Actual	0.82	0.80	0.83												
	Variance	0.02	(0.01)	0.01												
Headcount	Plan	755	755	755	740	740	740	680	680	700	730	750	680	750	750	750
(Effective #)	Actual	730	735	740												
	Variance	(25)	(20)	(15)												

Figure 3.13 – Example of a build-to-stock integrated business plan

As for the units of measure, having a same one to quantify demand, supply and inventory makes it more intuitive, easier to digest in relative terms. Example of common units include:

- Quantity: Number of items, units, pieces, pallets, etc.
- Weight: Kilograms, pounds, metric tons, etc.
- Volume: Litres, gallons, cubic meters, etc.
- Monetary Value: normally sales value.

However, there may be cases where different units are more appropriate due to the nature of the business or industry standards. In such cases, it's important to establish clear conversion factors and ensure that everyone involved understands how the units relate to each other.

The plan typically has four zones: past, firm, soft, and unconstrained. The past zone provides historical data and trends and may help validate the reasonableness of the plan going forward. The firm zone is typically characterized by high certainty because the orders or commitments are already in place. It consists of confirmed orders, contracts, or any other commitments that the organization has made to deliver products or services within a specific timeframe. The soft zone represents potential orders or sales that have a moderate level of certainty but are not yet firm commitments. The unconstrained zone represents the entire sales forecast without considering any resource limitations or constraints. It provides a high-level view of future demand trends and helps identify growth opportunities.

As illustrated in Figure 3.14, IBP goes through an ongoing cycle of structured meetings and analyses conducted at regular intervals to review and adjust the plan based on updated information, performance trends and changing conditions.

Figure 3.14 – Integrated Business Planning Cycle

This is typically on a monthly cycle as follows:

1. Week 1 - Demand Review: Validate the forecast based on updated market intelligence, customer feedback, and sales pipeline data. It may result in having to adjust the plan and strategies to make it happen.
2. Week 2 - Supply Review: Set the production plan to satisfy the demand to the extent possible based on resource availability, projected performance levels and business constraints.

3. Week 3 - Financial Review: Evaluate the financial implications of plan, including revenue projections, profit margin and cash-flow. Ensure that plan is aligned with financial goals, budgets, and targets set by the organization. Identify potential risks and uncertainties and develop mitigation strategies.
4. Week 4 - Reconciliation and Finalization: Consolidate the demand, supply, and financial plans into a single integrated plan. Make any final adjustments or refinements to the plan. Obtain approval from executive leadership for the final plan.

Initially, IBP can be a bumpy road. There will most likely be large variances to plan as you move forward. The key is to understand the reasons for these variances, take action to reduce where possible and keep fine tuning the plan… turning the wheel of plan-do-check-act.

Many organizations start doing IBP using Excel to bring all into one consolidated view. Excel can work for smaller or less complex organizations. For larger enterprises or those with more sophisticated planning needs, ERP systems can offer a more comprehensive and integrated solution. Systems such as Oracle, SAP and D365 provide comprehensive capabilities for financial planning, demand planning, supply chain planning, workforce planning, and more.

Chapter Summary / Key Takeaways

Plan Management involves the ongoing process of creating, implementing, monitoring, and adjusting a business plan to ensure that an organization successfully achieves its goals.

It involves answering five fundamental questions:

1. Where do we stand today?
2. Where do we want to be?
3. What are the barriers?
4. How will we overcome them?
5. Who must do what?

The current state is summarized in a SWOT, defining the organization's internal strengths and weaknesses as well as identifying external opportunities and threats.

The desired state is articulated as a vision and steered by strategic goals.

Barriers to achieve these goals are identified to then establish and prioritize the solutions to overcome them.

It involves applying a technique known as "Catchball" to open a dialogue at all levels of the organization in order to establish realistic targets supported by means to achieving them. X-matrices are used to weave the "Golden Thread" by which the goals and objectives of all teams can be traced to the organization's strategic goals.

Integrated business planning operationalizes an organization by aligning its structure, resources, and actions with its strategic goals. This comprehensive approach ensures that every part of the organization is working cohesively towards the desired outcomes, enhancing the likelihood of achieving the strategic vision efficiently and effectively.

In essence, Plan Management is about taking our bearings of our current position, establishing the destination of where we want to go, and charting the course to get there with everyone rowing in the same direction.

CHAPTER 4

Project Management

In the context of CIMS, Project Management involves planning and leading the delivery of the solutions that were identified as part of Plan Management.

A project, by definition, is a temporary endeavor undertaken to create a unique product, service, or result. It is defined by the tree dimensions of scope, time, and cost, often illustrated as a triangle.

In 1917, Henry Gantt developed the Gantt Chart, and modern project management was born. It has since evolved extensively and today there are several well-established frameworks and methodologies, and many with associated professional certifications.

I am certainly not offering a new framework or methodology in the domain of project management but will rather help bring into perspective where the more popular ones can come into play and complement each other. Simply put, we want to apply the best practices to:

- *Get It Done*
- *Do It Right*
- *Make It Stick*

It is under these three facets that can be slotted the well-established frameworks and methodologies as shown in Figure 4.1. This is not to suggest that they are only concerned about the facet under which they have been slotted but rather it represents their main area of competency.

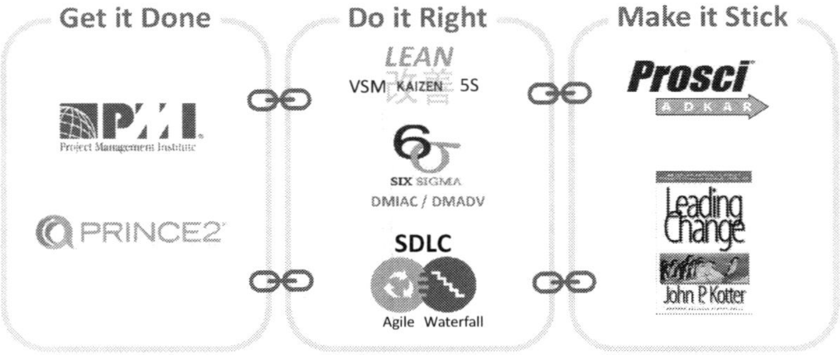

Figure 4.1 – Project Management Frameworks and Methodologies

Get it Done

Getting it done is about initiating, planning, executing, and controlling a project to its completion. This is project management in the purest sense. Figure 4.2 outlines the phases of project management`, which can be summarized by the saying: "*plan the work – work the plan*".

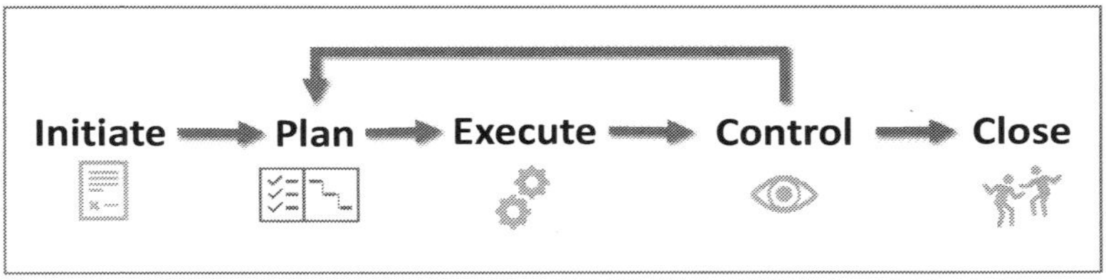

Figure 4.2 – Project Management Phases

The most widespread and adopted project management standards and best practices in the world are the PMBOK Guide and PRINCE2.

PMBOK which stands for "Project Management Body of Knowledge" was created by the Project Management Institute (PMI) founded in 1969 in the USA. PMI's first credential was the PMP (Project Management Professional) and remain very popular.

PRojects **IN** **C**ontrolled **E**nvironments or PRINCE2 has been in existence since 1989 and was organized by what is now known as OGC or the Office of Government Commerce in the UK. First utilized by the UK government as a process-based method of best project management practices, its methodologies are now utilized in many countries in Europe.

The PMP certification is preferred in America, Middle East and Australia. PRINCE2, however, is better recognized in Europe and Australia.

Figure 4.3 provides a comparison between PMBOK's area of knowledge and PRINCE2 themes.

PMBOK Guide Knowledge Areas	PRINCE2 themes
Project Integration Management	Business case, change, progress
Project Scope Management	Plans, progress
Project Schedule Management	Plans, progress
Project Cost Management	Plans, progress
Project Quality Management	Quality
Project Resource Management	Plans
Project Communications Management	Organization
Project Risk Management	Risk
Project Procurement Management	Not covered
Project Stakeholder Management	Organization

Figure 4.3 - PMBOK knowledge areas & PRINCE2 themes [6]

Each of these standards have their own merits, and in essence, each provide a solid approach to planning and controlling projects.

Do It Right

Doing it right is about applying the proper improvement and/or development methodologies that will most effectively deliver the solution.

For process improvement there are two main and well-established methodologies, namely Lean and Six Sigma.

Lean is focused on eliminating waste that target organizational efficiencies, while Six Sigma's focus is on eliminating defects and reducing variability. They both have several tools and techniques with very disciplined approaches. It is not necessarily one versus the other. In fact, the current trend is a blend of both, which is known as 'Lean Six Sigma'.

For software, system, or product development, the two basic most popular methodologies are Waterfall and Agile, both under the umbrella of SDLC – System Development Life Cycle.

Figure 4.4 summarizes the steps involved with both the Lean Six Sigma & SDLC methodologies.

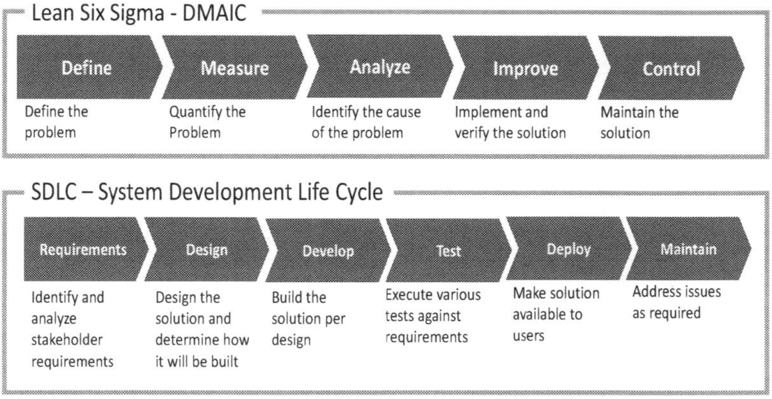

Figure 4.4 – Lean Six Sigma & SDLC methodologies

The Waterfall method is the conventional approach to product development, where a project is divided into sequential stages that must be completed in order. Agile takes an iterative approach to product development. Agile focuses on first producing a minimal viable product (MVP) and then improving with each iteration.

Figure 4.5 illustrates the difference between Waterfall and Agile product development.

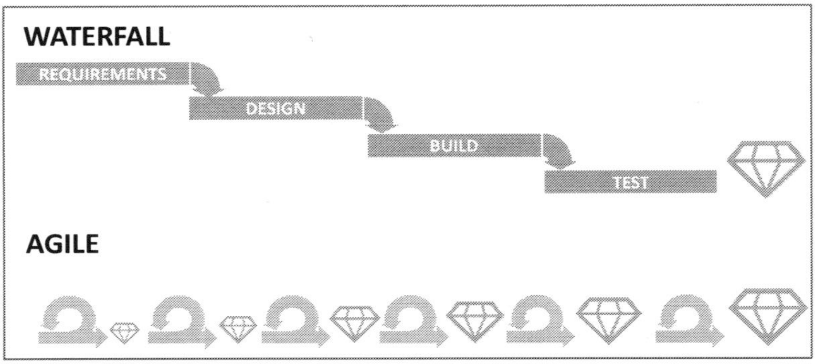

Figure 4.5 – Waterfall vs. Agile Product Development

Agile development is favored for pure development of new products where there is an element of uncertainty and innovation. The Agile methodology is based on four core values:

1. Individuals and interactions over processes and tools.
2. Working product over comprehensive documentation.
3. Customer collaboration over contract negotiation.
4. Responding to change over following a plan.

Agile development, which is illustrated in Figure 4.6, is an iterative development approach where requirements and solutions evolve through collaboration between self-organizing cross-functional teams. The method includes consecutive incremental steps called “sprint” coupled with “scrum” meetings including daily standups, sprint planning sessions, and sprint retrospectives.

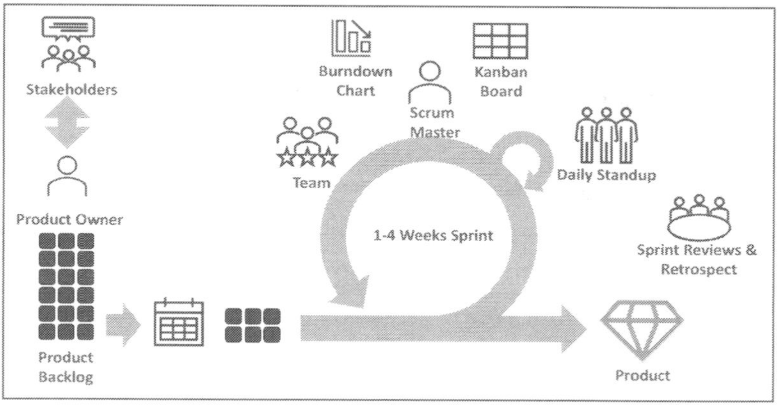

Figure 4.6 – Agile Product Development

And then, there is Wagile, which is a hybrid approach of both the Waterfall and Agile, also referred to as Water-Scrum-Fall.

Make It Stick

Making it stick is about ensuring that the introduction of changes that impact people is truly accepted, adopted, and sustained.

Project Management is the science of '*Get-it-Done*' on-time, within budget, and scope; while Organizational Change Management (OCM) is the social science of ensuring that the benefits of those projects are realized through the buy-in by the people who need to make it happen.

Two of the most common approaches in use today are John Kotter's 8-step method and Prosci's 3-phase method. Both are based on strong research models that aim to provide a basis for the systematic approach to managing the transition from current to future states.

Introduced in the 1995 book title "Leading Change", [7] the author and Harvard business professor John Kotter's 8-step process for change is a world-renowned methodology for transforming modern organizations. In a fast-paced world, keeping organizations relevant and efficient requires constant transformation and adjustment. Kotter's 8-step process is a great method for implementing and managing change in a way that can sustainably transform organizations. The following outlines the 8-step process:

1. Create a Sense of Urgency
2. Build a Guiding Coalition
3. Form a Strategic Vision and Initiatives
4. Enlist a Volunteer Army
5. Enable Action by Removing Barriers
6. Generate Short-Term Wins
7. Sustain Acceleration
8. Institute Change

The Prosci [8] approach is a goal-oriented change management model that guides individual and organizational change. Prosci defines change management as the application of a structured process and set of tools for leading the people side of change to achieve a desired outcome. It involves three phases:

1. Prepare for Change
2. Manage Change
3. Reinforce Change

Created by Prosci founder Jeff Hiatt, ADKAR is an acronym that represents the five tangible and concrete outcomes that people need to achieve for lasting change:

- **A**wareness of the need for change
- **D**esire to support the change
- **K**nowledge of how to change
- **A**bility to demonstrate skills and behavior
- **R**einforcement to make the change stick

One interesting aspect of Prosci is that it provides an effective way to measure the organizational readiness.

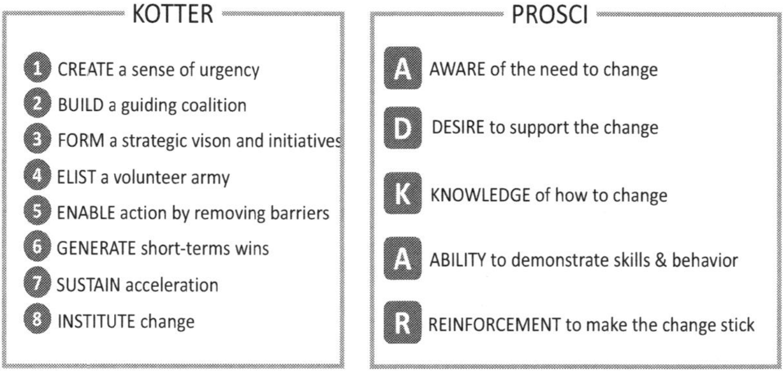

Figure 4.7 –Change Management Methodologies

I can personally attest to the effectiveness of these two methods because I have applied both as well as having felt the pain of not. The first transformational projects with which I was involved; we did not apply OCM simply because we knew nothing of it. As a young engineer, I simply thought that logic would prevail. But I came to realize that when you are asking people to change their ways, 2+2 may no longer equal 4. And then it is an uphill battle to get people to accept the change to achieve the expected results. But then, we did learn about OCM and applied it... lo and behold, it works!

Governance and Structure

Project governance and structure are essential components of any successful project delivery. A well-defined governance structure provides clarity on roles, responsibilities, and decision-making processes within the project. It ensures that everyone involved understands their role and how they contribute to the project's objectives. Figure 4.8 shows the project structure that reinforces the three facets of CIMS.

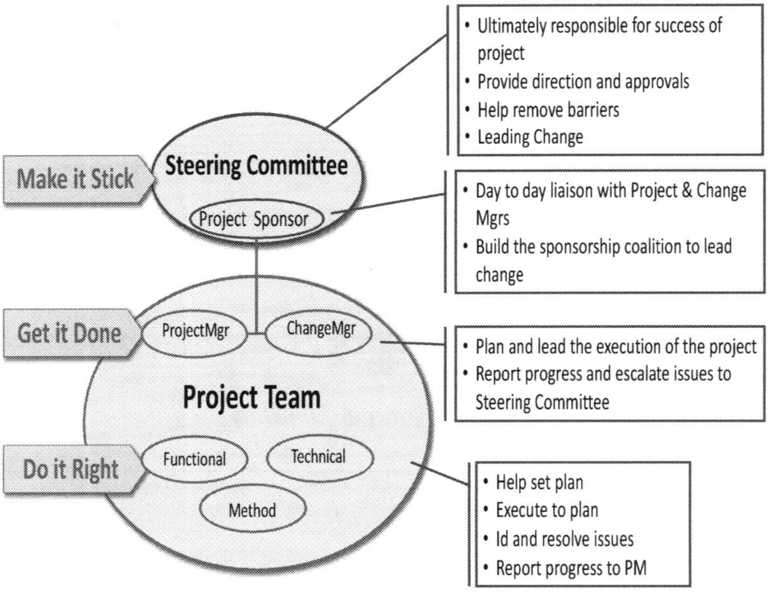

Figure 4.8 – Project Structure

The Steering Committee, also referred to as the Sponsoring Body, is the decision-making body ultimately responsible for the success of the project. It should be comprised of the key stakeholders who have authority over the project happenings and outcome.

The Steering Committee is not a forum to keep people in the loop or an advisory board. Being on this committee is not just about being involved but also being fully committed to the success of the project and help remove roadblocks.

A member of the committee is assigned as the Project Sponsor who is the day-to-day liaison with the project leadership. The sponsor champions the cause and builds the sponsorship coalition to lead the change within the organization or in other words '*make it stick'*.

The project team is responsible to plan and execute the project. It is comprised of the resource required to '*get it done*' and '*do it right*'. This includes project and change manager(s) as well as subject matter experts (SME's) in the various areas of competencies required, i.e., functional, technical and methods.

The Project Manager is responsible to plan and lead the execution ('*get it done*') and reports progress to the Steering Committee, as well as escalate issues and seek direction and approvals.

The Change Manager guides and supports the business leadership to lead the change ('*make it stick*') and monitors the business readiness.

The Project Manager and Change Manager normally work together. The Project Manager mainly focuses on internal activities within the team, whereas the Change Manager mainly focuses on external activities.

It is important to note that it is not the responsibility of the Project Team to '*make it stick*'. The Project Team will support the effort, such as developing and delivering training. But it truly lies with the leaders of the organization to lead the change and get employees on board. The role of the Change Manager is to prepare, coach and support the leaders in leading the change.

The SME's on the project team collectively own '*doing it right*'. The functional SMEs are normally employees who come from the business functions that are impacted by the solution, and they will want to ensure that the new solution satisfies the business needs. The technical SMEs would include experts of the technologies that are used to enable the solution. And finally, the methods SME's guide and support the team through the applicable methodologies (i.e., Lean, Six Sigma, SDLC).

Project Charter

A project charter is essential for laying the foundation for a successful project, providing clarity, direction, and alignment among stakeholders, and setting the stage for effective project execution and control. It clearly defines the objective, scope, deliverables, and responsibilities of the project with estimated timeline and cost in consideration of stipulated assumptions and constraints. It serves as a baseline for monitoring and controlling the project, meaning that it provides a reference point for monitoring milestones and cost, tracking changes, and evaluating the overall success of the project against its original goals and objectives. A template of a project charter is shown in Figure 4.9.

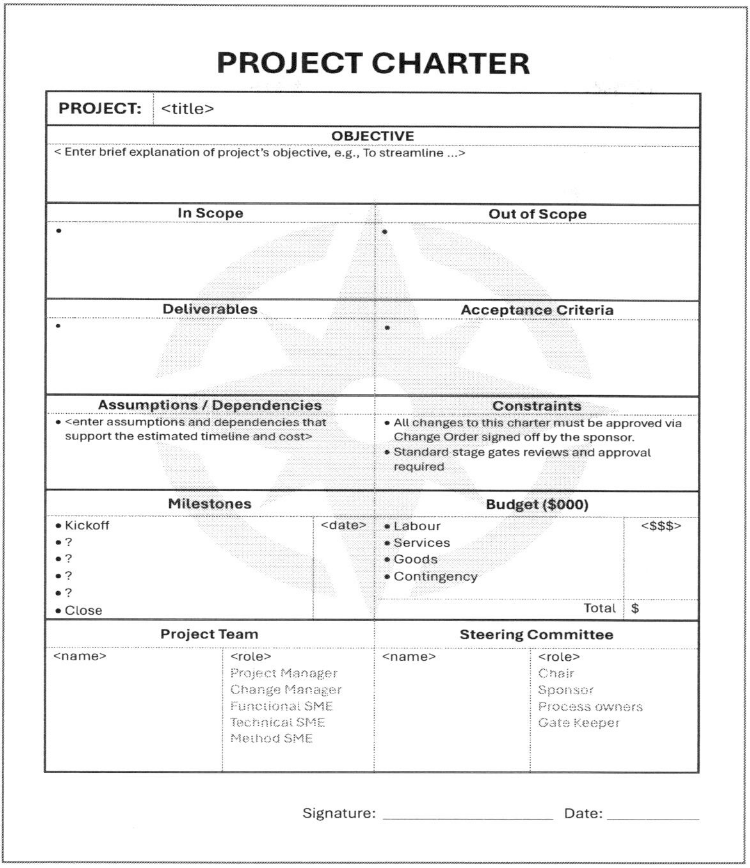

PROJECT CHARTER

PROJECT: <title>

OBJECTIVE

< Enter brief explanation of project's objective, e.g., To streamline ...>

In Scope	Out of Scope
•	•

Deliverables	Acceptance Criteria
•	•

Assumptions / Dependencies	Constraints
• <enter assumptions and dependencies that support the estimated timeline and cost>	• All changes to this charter must be approved via Change Order signed off by the sponsor. • Standard stage gates reviews and approval required

Milestones		Budget ($000)	
• Kickoff • ? • ? • ? • ? • Close	<date>	• Labour • Services • Goods • Contingency	<$$$>
		Total	$

Project Team		Steering Committee	
<name>	<role> Project Manager Change Manager Functional SME Technical SME Method SME	<name>	<role> Chair Sponsor Process owners Gate Keeper

Signature: ____________________ Date: ___________

Figure 4.9 – Project Charter

Project Plan

Too often, project managers come with ready-baked plans and present them to the team as a 'tell' and not an 'ask' … not a great way to create engagement, nor to leverage the expertise within the team.

I would therefore suggest that we want to create a project plan in a participative way to create engagement as well as draw on the experience and expertise of the team members. This is done by simply having a brainstorming session with the team, as follows:

1. Define the project's expected outcome (i.e., final deliverables).
2. Brainstorm the activities to make it happen.
3. Affinitize – group activities into summary activities.
4. Establish inter-dependencies between summary activities.
5. Define timeframe for each summary activity.
6. Assign ownership to each summary activity.
7. Create Gantt Chart schedule.
8. Identify potential risks and counteractions.

Steps 2 to 4, which involves using sticky-notes and posting them on a wall, are illustrated in Figure 4.10.

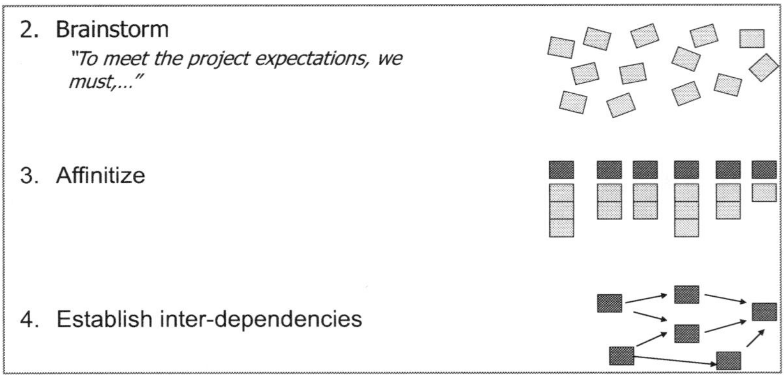

Figure 4.10 – Brainstorming tasks to Get It Done

The Project Manager now has what it takes to finalize the project plan and obtain the proper approvals to get on with it. Once approved, the plan is baselined, hence the budget of scope, time, and cost against which progress will be reported.

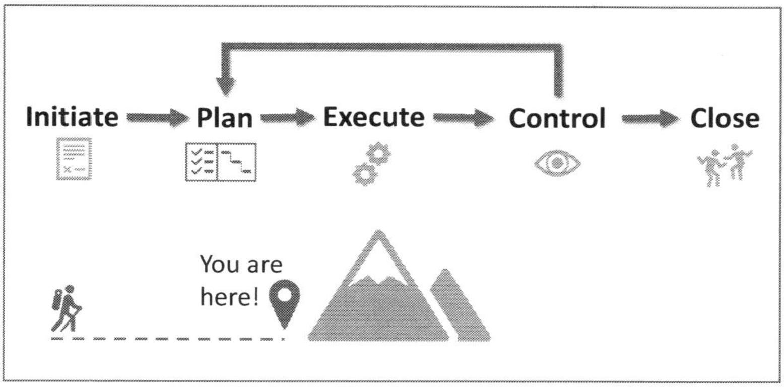

Figure 4.11 – Ready to Execute per Plan

And now the team can move on with the execution phase as illustrated in Figure 4.11. In doing so, the team must remain true to the plan, recognizing however that the plan is a living document, meaning that it needs to be kept up to date and adjusted as required to reflect the realities of the project. As the project moves forward there will be challenges and unforeseen circumstances to contend with. There will most likely need to be some 'bob and weaving' to make it through to the end.

Here are suggested rules of engagement for the team in executing the project:

1. Begin with the end in mind.
2. Work as a team…help each other.
3. Do not let perfection get in the way of progress.

4. Attack the problem not the person.
5. Be flexible and nimble in your response to obstacles.
6. Keep plan current… adjust as required.
7. Celebrate your wins.

Stage Gating Approach

A stage gate process, also known as a phase-gate process, is a project management technique that divides an initiative or project into distinct stages or phases. These stages are separated by decision points, referred to as gates. At each gate, continuation is decided normally by the steering committee. It is intended to ensure that the business case still stands to support the investment and that the team is well positioned to proceed with the next stage or phase of the project.

Here are the five stage gates that I am proposing:

1. <u>Start</u>: Do we have all our 'ducks in order' to fully engage the execution of the project?
2. <u>Solution</u>: Have we thoroughly understood the problem/requirements before proceeding with solutioning/designing?
3. <u>Buy/Build</u>: Does the solution effectively address the problem/satisfy the requirements before committing to purchase and/or build it? Does the business case still hold based on the estimated cost and timeline for full implementation?

4. Implement: Has the solution been thoroughly tested and have users been properly trained. Are we ready to deploy the solution / go-live?
5. Close: Has the solution been properly implemented? Are proper controls in place to support and sustain the solution? Can the project be closed, and project team disbanded?

It is important to understand that a stage gate is not an exit point but rather an entry point into the next phase except for the very last one. Figure 4.12 illustrates where gates would apply for either sequential or overlapping stages.

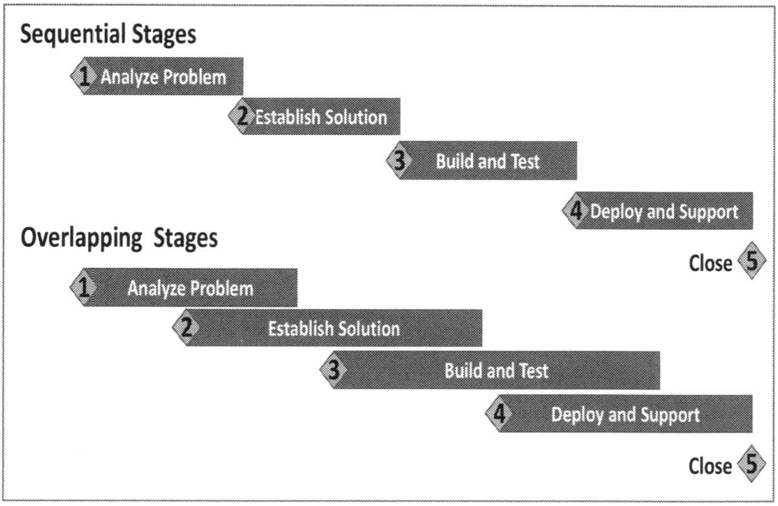

Figure 4.12 – Project Stage Gates

Probably the most important stage gate review is the very first one. Too often, projects start with too many loose ends and quickly get into trouble. A major project fully ready to start would meet the following criteria:

a) The project objectives, scope and deliverables are clear and agreed to.

b) The Steering Committee is comprised of senior leadership representing the areas affected by the change.

c) The Project Sponsor has the proper level of credibility and authority.

d) The Project Manager and Change Manager have the proper level of experience to lead the execution of the project.

e) The Project Team is comprised of the proper business, technical and applicable method SME's (subject matter experts).

f) The approach used to manage and execute the project is documented, well understood, and approved.

g) The project timeline and cost estimate are deemed as being reasonably achievable.

h) There are no known conflicts or significant risks that would prevent proceeding with the project.

Chapter Summary / Key Takeaways

Project Management involves planning and leading the delivery of the solutions that were identified as part of Plan Management.

CIMS is not proposing any new methodologies for solution delivery, but rather is promoting an integrated approach to applying leading practices, under the following three facets:

- *Get It Done*
- *Do it Right*
- *Make it Stick*

The project's Steering Committee is ultimately responsible for the success of a project, and in leading the organizational change… '*Make It Stick!*'.

The Project and Change Manager(s) are responsible to plan and lead the execution… '*Get It Done!*'.

And the project team is comprised of functional, technical and methodology SME's (subject matter experts) who are collectively responsible to '*Do It Right!*'.

A project charter is essential for laying the foundation for a successful project, providing clarity, direction, and alignment among stakeholders, and setting the stage for effective project execution and control.

Recognizing that projects can represent significant investments, stage gating should be used to validate at specific points of the project that the business case still stands and that it is well positioned to keep moving forward.

CHAPTER 5

Progress Management

Progress Management, which is akin to what is generally known as Daily Management, involves monitoring progress throughout the organization and engaging employees to identify and action improvement opportunities. It is about 'keeping your eye on the ball', making sure the work gets done properly and in a timely manner, while seeking to continuously improve and not allowing gains to backslide.

"The way a team plays as a whole determines its success. You may have the greatest bunch of individual stars in the

world, but if they don't play together, the club won't be worth a dime." Babe Ruth, the legendary baseball player

Make It Visual

When you go to a sporting event such as hockey, baseball, or football, you can tell at a glance who is winning and losing the game by simply looking at the scoreboard. They are just numbers, but yet they create so much passion with both the players and the spectators.

In the same spirit, we want to make the performance of the team in the workplace visible at a glance. This is normally in the form of a visibility board with key performance indicators (KPI's) as illustrated in Figure 5.1. A good method of clearly indicating if the metric is heading in the right or wrong direction is to use the traffic light indicators; green, yellow, or red to respectively indicate that the progress is favorable, lagging or unfavorable.

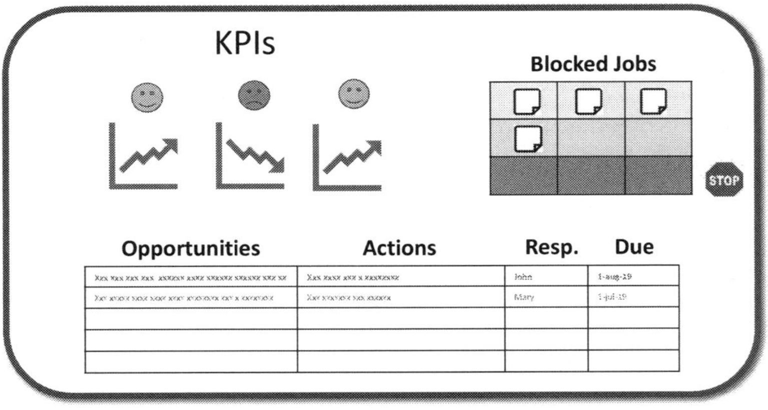

Figure 5.1 – Team Visibility Board

Progress Meetings

If nothing else, holding regular team meetings serves as a reminder to everyone that they are indeed part of a team and not isolated. Working together to set goals is a critical part of any organization's success. It is, therefore, important to have regular meetings so that the team can have an overall view of the team's progress. When done well, these meetings will help improve the general performance of the team and the productivity of individual members.

These progress meetings are the "Check/Act" of the Plan-Do-Check-Act (PDCA) cycle. Progress is reviewed with the team to identify improvement opportunities and deploy action. They need to occur at a frequency that maintains proper momentum, normally at the same cadence as the PDCA cycle. For instance, the front line may hold daily meetings, while management would normally meet weekly. The upper management may choose to have a rotating agenda reviewing each week progress against different metrics (e.g., cost, quality, delivery, safety, and morale).

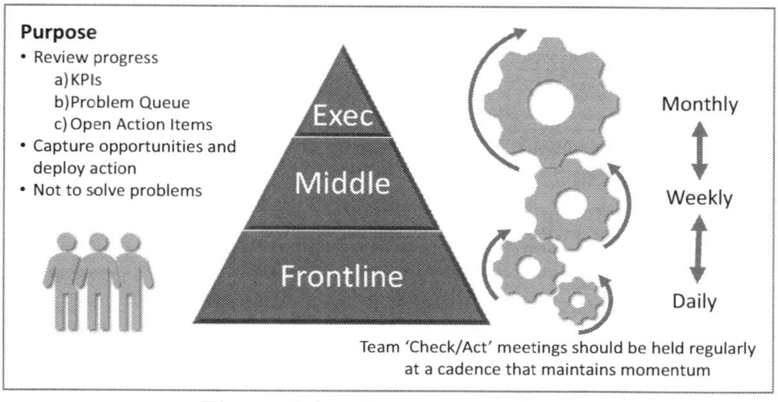

Figure 5.2 – Progress Meetings

The progress meetings, however, are not intended to be problem-solving sessions. If there is a problem to be solved, then it would be captured as an opportunity and action would be deployed to resolve it. And, if necessary, this can involve holding a separate meeting with who needs to be involved, which most likely would not be the whole team.

The progress meetings should be short and sweet. The front-line daily meetings should be 15 minutes or so. They should be held as a standup meeting in front of the visibility board. Middle Management meetings would normally be ½ to 1 hour at the most. In the case of management meetings, they would not normally have a visibility board but would nonetheless review key performance indicator projected on a screen and maintain an opportunity sheet. A sample template of an opportunity sheet is shown in Figure 5.3.

Opportunity	Priority	Action	Resp.	Due	Status
Problem statement (not an action or assumed solution)	H,M,L	Task (verb & known)	Who from team	~~Original Date~~ Revised Date	

Figure 5.3 – Opportunity Sheet template

In order to instill ownership, the team leader in the Progress meetings needs to more so 'ask' than 'tell'. It is about seeking input from the team on their progress and their ideas on how to improve. In essence, it is about leading the team with questions.

Attack the Problem not the Person

It only takes one drop of vinegar to ruin a good bottle of wine. Shedding blame is the one drop of vinegar to teamwork.

Doctor W. Edwards Deming, globally regarded as the father of the quality revolution, stated that "I should estimate that in my experience most troubles and most possibilities for improvement add up to the proportions something like this: 94% belongs to the system (responsibility of management) and 6% special." [9]

It is therefore important that when confronted with problems, that the leadership guide the team to always attack the problem and not the person. Or another way of saying it: "Blame the process, not the person".

To set the right mindset, I would suggest that the term "opportunity" be used instead of "problem".

Five Whys

In 'attacking the problems' it is important that we deal with the root cause, otherwise the problem will most likely resurface.

A Lean technique that came from Toyota, known as "5 Whys", is an iterative interrogative technique used to explore the cause-and-effect relationships underlying a particular problem. The primary goal of the technique is to identify the root cause of a defect or problem by repeatedly asking "Why?" Each answer serves as the foundation for the subsequent question. Here is a simple example.

1. Our on-time delivery has been dropping. Why?
2. Products from Supplier X are often damaged, causing delays. Why?
3. Products are damaged in transit. Why?
4. Packaging is not properly protecting it. Why?
5. We do not provide specs for packaging. Why?
6. We assume that our vendors have the expertise.

Six Sigma practitioners would normally come into play for more complex problems, where the answer to some of the whys would require more of scientific approach to establishing and quantifying the true causes.

Stop the Line

A well-known quality control mechanism, from Toyota as well, is the Andon cord. The cord serves as a means to alert others about issues on the production line. Pulling the cord immediately halts production, signaling that a critical issue requires an immediate response. It gives the worker the ability, and more importantly, the empowerment, to halt production when a defect is found and promptly request assistance.

The 'stop the line' concept has been implemented across many sectors as a policy, empowering employees to stop work under specific circumstances normally tied to quality and safety. It has proven to be beneficial in addressing problems quickly, increasing quality, improving safety, augmenting employee engagement, and improving customer satisfaction.

A practical method for implementing the 'stop the line' concept involves ensuring that blocked tasks are highly visible in the workplace and setting a limit on the number that can be tolerated before action is taken. This can be achieved by establishing a queue with three zones: green, yellow, and red. Employees should prioritize resolving blockers promptly. If the number of blocked tasks enters the yellow zone, the team leader should be notified for assistance. If it escalates to the red zone, the team leader's leader must also be engaged for further support. Once the red zone reaches its limit, employees must halt operations and seek guidance from leadership. Only senior leadership can authorize work to resume while corrective actions are implemented. Additionally, the team should maintain a tally of the causes of blockages to identify systemic issues and opportunities for improvement. Over time, the goal should be to systematically reduce the limit on blocked tasks, aiming for an ideal of one, as practiced at Toyota.

Standardize Work

By documenting the best way known to execute a process, it forms the baseline for continuous improvement. As the standard improves, the new standard sets the baseline for further enhancements, continuing the cycle of improvement in standardized work. It leverages the learnings and ensures that the gains are sustained, i.e., no backsliding.

Standardizing work involves documenting and adhering to a detailed breakdown of the steps to follow in order to produce a product or perform a service in the most efficient and effective way known. These work instructions should be created and maintained by the team members. Ideally these work instructions should be visible in the workplace or easily accessible at point of use.

5S+1 Roadmap to the Visual Workplace

5S+1 is a methodology for organizing the workplace that originated from Japan in the manufacturing sector. It involves exercising activities that are summarized into five Japanese words, which have been translated as follows:

Japanese	English
Seiri	Sort or Separate
Seiton	Simplify or Set in Order
Seiso	Sweep or Shine
Seiketsu	Standardize or Schedule
Shitsuke	Self-discipline or Sustain

"+1" was subsequently added for "Safety".

The following briefly outlines what each entail:

- SORT: Keep only necessary items in the workplace.
- SIMPLIFY: Arrange items to promote efficient workflow.
- SWEEP: Clean the work area so it is neat and tidy
- STANDARDIZE: Set standards for a consistently organized workplace.
- SELF-DISCIPLINE: Make 5S a habit and continually improve.

- +1 SAFETY: Ensure area is free of hazardous or dangerous conditions.

Although 5S+1 started in manufacturing, it is now commonly applied worldwide in many other sectors e.g., healthcare, retail, warehousing, service, and construction.

When done right, it creates the Visual Workplace where waste and abnormal conditions can be seen at a glance. It provides clear visual cues and standardized processes for employees to follow.

Initially, 5S+1 is most effectively implemented by conducting a Kaizen Blitz (Rapid Improvement Event) in the workplace involving the employees. The evaluation sheet shown in Figure 5.4 can help monitor and reinforce progress moving forward.

5S+1 LEVELS

	1 -Poor	2 - Marginal	3 - Good	4 - Very Good	5 - Excellent
SORT	Mixture of unneeded and needed items in the area, or work area is cluttered.	A partial sort has taken place, and unneeded items have been RED tagged. Remains somewhat cluttered.	Most unneeded items have been removed from the area and unneeded items are RED tagged.	Only needed items remain in the area.	Only needed items remain, and process controls are in place to prevent any unneeded items from re-entering the area.
SIMPLIFY	Several items are stored in a random fashion without visual controls. Or it is difficult to determine if anything is out of place.	Most items have a designated place with some form of visual control (i.e. labels, floor lines, min/max lines, shadow boards, outlines, colors).	Most items have a designated place with clear visual controls (i.e., labels, floor lines, min/max lines, shadow boards, outlines, colors).	All items have a place. visual controls define item locations, min/max, work area boundaries, etc.	A true visual workplace! *"A place for everything and everything in its place."* And any abnormalities are visible-at-a-glance!
SWEEP	Dirty area with no evidence of systematic cleaning. Or Many items are dirty and in poor condition. Many items are not in their designated place.	Area is fairly clean. However, routine cleaning is not in evidence. Or Visual Sweeps are not regularly done to identify items requiring attention.	Most items in the area are clean. And Visual Sweeps are done regularly to identify items requiring attention.	Regular cleaning and inspection of the workplace is clearly evident. And area is clean, free of clutter, and in good condition.	A spotless, inviting environment with careful attention to detail. And objective evidence of daily Visual Sweep.

Figure 5.4 – 5S+1 Level (1/2)

STANDARDIZE	How goods flow in, within and out of the area is not documented. Or no 5S to-do list.	Some labeling and instructions implemented with respect to 5S activities and flow of goods. And 5S To-Do list initiated and posted	Most of regular 5S activities documented. And how goods flow in, within and out of the area is mostly documented with instructions and labels that can be seen at a glance.	All 5S activities and flow of goods are well documented and can be seen at a glance.	Primary focus is prevention. And Standards are continuously being enhanced to implement "mistake-proofing" techniques.
SELF-DISCIPLINE	Most employees are not complying with 5S procedures. Or there is little evidence of management follow-up, coaching and support.	Some employees are complying with 5S. Or some management follow-through. Many opportunities for improvement.	Process is regularly monitored and, for the most part, 5S disciplines are being adhered to. And opportunities are being documented with mgt follow-up.	Compliance is very good. Mgt and employees are actively monitoring and improving the process.	5S is embraced as an integral part of daily operations. And compliance is a way of life. And deviations from the process are quickly identified and remedied.
SAFETY	Accidents/incidents regularly occur Or PPE generally not worn. Or Safe Work Practices (SWP's) nor adhered to. Or several hazards exist.	PPE req't posted and normally worn. And WHMIS data is up-to-date and available in the area.	Employees are not unduly exposed to hazards in the area. PPE and SWP's, are posted and adhered to. And WHMIS data is up-to-date and readily available. And the evacuation plan is clearly posted in the area. And no accidents since last audit	Same as 3 plus: No hazard notice issued by JOHSC during last audit and none still open from previous audits. And no accidents in last 3 months	Safety consciousness is a way of life. There has been no hazard notice issued or outstanding for the past 6 months. And no accidents reported for the past 6 six months.

Figure 5.4 – 5S+1 Level (2/2)

Virtual Teams

Having team players working remotely has been an increasing reality, accelerated by the advent of the coronavirus pandemic, which forced many organizations to quickly adapt to having a large portion of their workforce working from home. Fortunately, the technology was at the rendezvous to make it happen with the likes of Microsoft Teams, Zoom, Google Meet and many other collaborative applications.

So, what does this mean for Progress Management? The fundamentals remain the same in terms of having to engage employees to work as a team with a common purpose with a sense of belonging. The media, however, would change from being physical to digital. The visibility boards for instance would go from being physical to digital boards.

The key here is for the leader to bring the team together, aligned everyone to a common purpose. Admittedly it is more challenging to do this with remote workers. If anything, it requires more touchpoints by having daily team huddles and frequent one-on-one with each of the team members.

Figure 5.5 outlines suggested rules of engagement (STARS) for the virtual team meetings.

- Be **S**avvy… leverage the collaboration tools
- Be **T**here… turn on the camera
- Be **A**ttentive… no multitasking
- Be **R**espectful… raise your hand
- Be **S**ocial… Happy Birthday!

Figure 5.5 – Virtual Meeting Rules of Engagement

Chapter Summary / Key Takeaways

Progress Management is used to ensure that the organization is continually moving forward by incrementally improving its processes. It is about 'keeping your eye on the ball', making sure the work gets done properly and in a timely manner, while seeking to continuously improve and not allowing gains to backslide.

It involves making progress visible in the workplace and engaging employees in continuously seeking improvements.

5S+1 is a workplace organization methodology which is a proven roadmap to create the visual workplace where waste and abnormal conditions can be seen at a glance. It provides clear visual cues and standardized processes for employees to follow.

Work is standardized by documenting and adhering to a detailed breakdown of the steps to follow in order to produce a product or perform a service in the most efficient and effective way known. Documenting the current best practices, standardized work establishes the foundation for continuous improvement.

Progress Management includes having an escalation process for when too many jobs are held by problems to a point that the work will be stopped to address the so-called "blockers".

Attack the problem and not the person… problems need to be viewed as opportunities and not failures.

When it comes to virtual teams, change the media but not the mode.

CHAPTER 6

Process Management

Foundational to Continuous Improvement, Process Management is a method to select, organize, and manage the improvement and standardization of business processes.

A Process is a set of activities that interact to produce a result. Most things we do in business can be defined or thought of as a process. Processes cut across functions, departments, and organizations. Quality is a result of reliable processes and methods. It is better to build quality upstream in the process than to try to control quality downstream.

To effectively manage processes, there needs to be clear ownership and governance. The processes need to be standardized and measured in order to become a baseline for continuous improvement.

A process that is standardized means that it is documented and adhered to. Standardization of the business processes involves creating and maintaining operating policies, procedures and work instructions.

Operating policies set direction and clear ownership. Procedures describe the steps to be followed in compliance with these policies. And work instructions further detail how these procedural steps are to be performed. The hierarchy is illustrated in Figure 6.1.

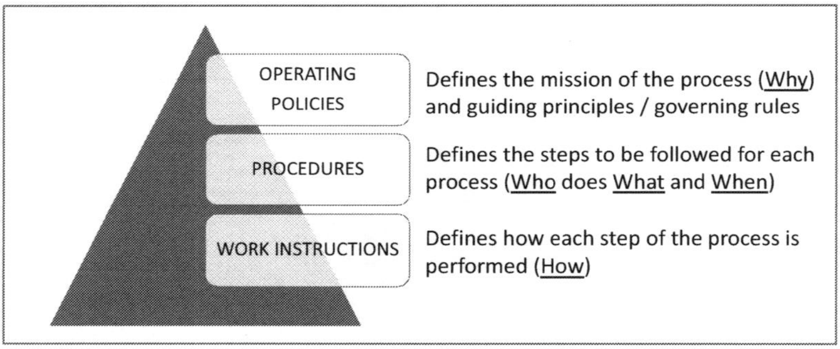

Figure 6.1 – Process Classification Framework

The implementation and continuation of Process Management involves the steps as outlined in Figure 6.2 and further explained below.

Figure 6.2 – Implementing Process Management

Process Management Standards

Firstly, standards should be set in order to ease the communication and collaboration across the organization. This should include the following:

1. Template for policies, normally in the form of a written document.
2. Template for procedures, normally in the form of swimlane diagrams.
3. Work instructions, normally in form of written document or checklist with illustrations, screenshots, etc.
4. KPI format, normally in form of trend chart
5. Visibility / Dashboard layout.
6. Guidelines on use of traffic light indicators.
7. Software application(s) to enable the above.

A lot of this can be satisfied by leveraging existing industry standards and best practices. In fact, there is the Association of Business Process Management Professionals (ABPMP), which is a non-profit vendor independent professional organization dedicated to the advancement of business process management concepts and its practices. [10]

Model the Business

Creating a tier 1 process map and categorizing the sub-processes under each tier (tier 2 and, where applicable, tier 3) is part of business modeling. In essence, this defines the work breakdown structure of the organization, also known as a 'process classification framework'. Figure 6.3 shows an example of a tier 1 process map.

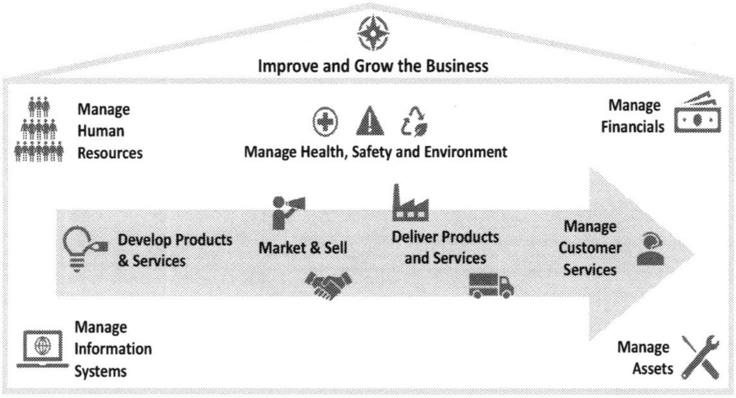

Figure 6.3 – Example of Tier 1 Process Map

In this example, the processes in the arrow would be considered as the value stream, hence deliver value to the customer. ChatGPT

The processes outside the arrow within the rectangle are the enabling processes, and the one at the peak is the leadership process, where CIMS resides.

Here too existing material can be leveraged. For instance, APQC (American Productivity & Quality Center) is a member-based and non-profit organization, which defines and maintains process classification frameworks (PCF) for various types of industries. APQC conducts research to discover and document world-class business practices, share proven methodologies and processes, and assist organizations around the world in adapting them. The PCF creates a common language by outlining all processes practiced by most organizations, categorizing them, and aligning them according to a hierarchical numbering system. [11] Figure 6.4 depicts an example of APQC tier 1 processes.

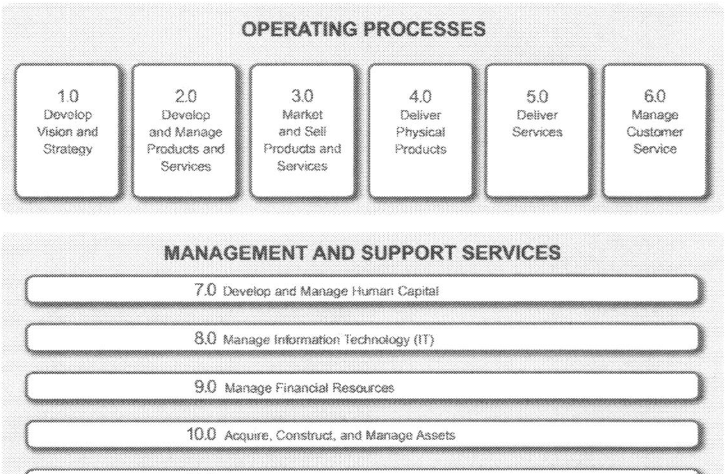

Figure 6.4 – APQC Process Classification Framework

Process Ownership

The process owner is responsible for standardizing and optimizing their processes in alignment with the broader organizational goals. It does not mean however that the sub-process owners or employees executing the process necessarily report organizationally under the process owner. For instance, the head of Human Resources may own the performance review process, but the execution of this process falls with all the management and employees.

Each process must be assigned a process owner. An individual can be the owner of several processes, but it is generally preferable to have only one process owner for a given process, ensuring a single point of accountability and consistent decision-making.

For tier 1 level processes, the ownership should be at executive level of the organization. In most cases, this is obvious. For instance, the head of finance would own "Manage Financial Resources". On the other hand, some other processes may not be so obvious and will require some consideration as to who in the senior management team is best suited to assume ownership.

Normally the tier 1 process owners form the Process Council to oversee and guide the optimization of business processes across the organization. This includes ensuring alignment with strategic objectives, identifying and eliminating inefficiencies, promoting cross-functional collaboration, and fostering continuous improvement to enhance overall operational performance and customer satisfaction.

Operating Policies

To ensure proper alignment to the organization's vision, values and strategic goals, an operating policy should be established for each of the tier 1 processes.

The operating policies should be drafted by the process owners and then presented to the executive team for approval.

An operating policy should include the following:

- Purpose of the process
- Key Performance Indicators (KPI's)
- Policy statements
- Associated roles and responsibilities

A sample template is shown in Figure 6.5.

By clearly articulating the purpose of the process, the policy provides a comprehensive understanding of why the process is important and how it contributes to the overall success of the organization. This clarity helps ensure that everyone involved understands the significance of their roles and responsibilities within the process.

Key Performance Indicators (KPIs) for a tier 1 process are the upper metrics that help measure the effectiveness and efficiency of the process. These KPIs should validate that the stated purpose of the process is being fulfilled.

The policy statements are guiding principles (should) and governing rules (must). They set direction and boundaries, but do not describe how the process is executed. The latter falls in the domain of procedures and work instructions. For instance, there may be a policy under Manage Customer Services that states: "Customer returns shall be accepted within 30 days of purchase". The procedure would then describe how the process is to be executed to comply with this policy.

Associated roles and responsibilities defined within the policy documents are again not prescribing how to perform the process, but rather the duties and obligations of the applicable roles as it relates to each tier 1 process. Responsibilities would normally start with verbs such as "assure", "ensure", "approve" and "oversee".

It is important to note that these policies are not set in stone. They themselves are subject to continuous improvement and should therefore be reviewed periodically and revised as necessary to keep the organization aligned with strategic goals. Typically, all policies should undergo an annual review.

ABC Company

Operating Policy

No: 001 Rev 0
Date

PROCESS: verb & noun

PURPOSE: To ...

OWNER: Title

KPIs:

Effectiveness
- ?

Efficiency
- ?

POLICY STATEMENTS

A. ?
B. ?
C. ?
D. ?

RESPONSIBILITIES

1. **Role A**
   a. Ensure...
   b. Approve...
   c. Etc.
2. **Role B**
   a. Ensure...
   b. Approve...
   c. Etc.
3. **Etc.**

APPENDICES

i. ?
ii. ?
iii. ?

Figure 6.5 –Operating Policy sample template

Key Performance Indicators (KPIs)

CIMS Principle #2: *What Gets Measured, Gets Done*. Or another way of saying it: "What doesn't get measured, doesn't get managed".

So, to manage and improve processes we need to implement Key Performance Indicators (KPIs), and normally from two perspectives: effectiveness and efficiency.

Effectiveness involves successfully accomplishing a task or achieving a desired outcome. It emphasizes *doing the right things* to produce the intended results.

Efficiency, on the other hand, pertains to executing a task in the optimal manner possible. It involves *doing things in the right way* to complete tasks using minimal time, effort, and resources.

Examples of effectiveness and efficiency metrics are shown in Figure 6.6.

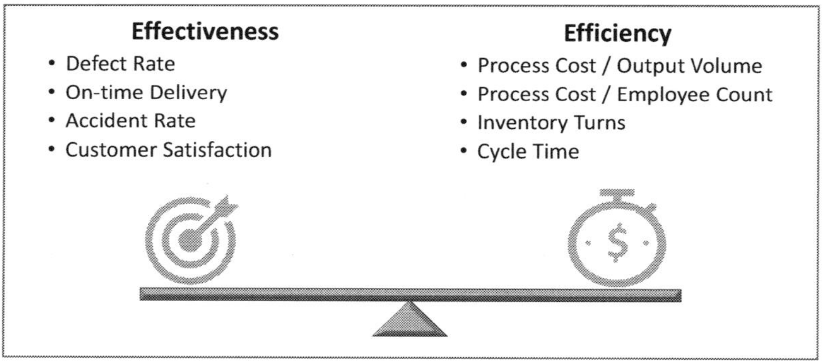

Figure 6.6 – Process Measures

Note that APQC is also a good source for obtaining industry leading KPI's and benchmarking data. [11]

Having KPIs implemented means that they are clearly visible in the workplace (physical and virtual) and are used to validate that the processes are performing as expected or otherwise help identify improvement opportunities.

The visual representation of the KPIs is also very important. One should be able to see the trend over time as compared to the target. Figure 6.7 shows how a KPI can be presented from bad to better to best.

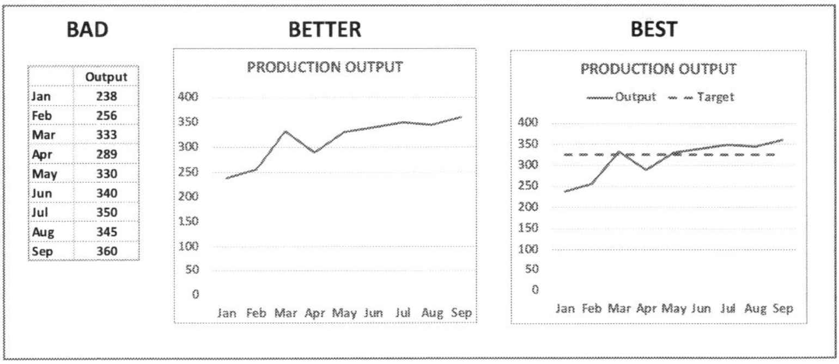

Figure 6.7 – Presentation of Performance Indicator

Accompanying trend charts with pareto charts is also a good practice to help identify where the greatest opportunities exist. In the example of a pareto chart shown in Figure 6.8, causes A, B, C and D account for over 80% of the defects. So, this is where the improvement efforts should focus. Then one can apply the 5 Whys technique on each of these causes to uncover the root cause... CIM Principle #2, *A Problem Well Understood is Half Solved.*

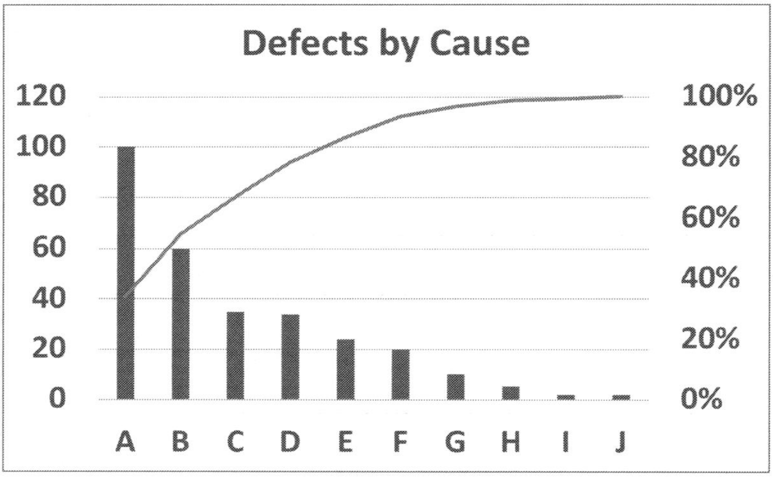

Figure 6.8 – Pareto Chart example

Selecting Processes… to Attack!

The goal of Process Management is not to standardize processes merely for the sake of standardization, but rather to improve processes in order to achieve strategic goals. Standardizing is simply a step towards achieving the expected improvements and holding the gains. Therefore, we are not going to standardize processes for the purpose of standardizing processes. Instead, we want to 'attack' the processes that will have the greatest impact on achieving the strategic goals. This can be accomplished by assessing the improvement opportunities of the tier 2 processes relative to the strategic goals. In other words, where can we get the 'biggest bang for our buck'?

Opportunities to improve processes can be established through benchmarking against industry best practices. And then we can identify how adopting best practices would contribute to achieving our strategic goals.

Figure 6.9 shows an example of an impact assessment, which can help prioritize processes to 'attack'. The processes are first evaluated in terms of their potential improvement opportunity using a scale of 0 to 4, 1 being minor and 4 being major. And then, this potential improvement is evaluated in terms of the impact it would have on each of the strategic goals, using the same scale. The overall impact is equal to the improvement opportunity multiplied by the sum of the impact against each strategic goal. In this example, 'build product' not only has the greatest improvement opportunity but also has the greatest overall impact on strategic goals.

○ 0 ◔ 1 ◑ 2 ◕ 3 ● 4

			STRATEGIC GOALS				
Process	Potential	x	Customer Experience	On-time Delivery	Quality	Employee Engagement	Impact
Design product	◑	x	◔	○	◑	◔	8
Build product	◕	x	○	●	●	◕	33
Market product	◑	x	◑	◔	○	○	6
Sell product	◔	x	●	◔	○	○	5
Deliver product	◑	x	◕	●	◔	○	16
Service product	◑	x	●	○	◔	◔	12

Figure 6.9 – Process Improvement Impact Assessment

Improve and Standardize Processes

Process improvements are driven by Progress Management and Project Management as illustrated in Figure 6.10. Progress Management is used to drive incremental process improvements, while Project Management drives the more significant 'step change' improvements.

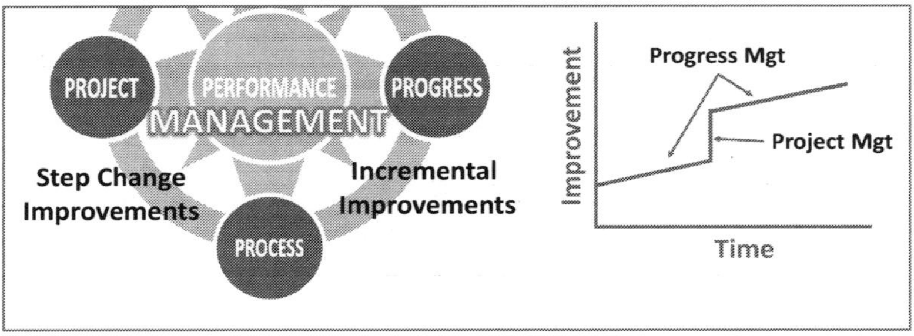

Figure 6.10 – Process Improvement driven by Project and Progress Management

Just by mapping the 'as-is' process, more often than not, obvious improvements come to light (i.e., 'low hanging fruits'), which would fall under the realm of "just do it". Then the Lean and Six Sigma methodologies can come into play to reap further improvements. Lean is about exposing and removing waste (non-value-added activities), whereas Six Sigma is about reducing variation. Figure 6.11 illustrates where these methods apply in terms of bearing the fruits of process improvement.

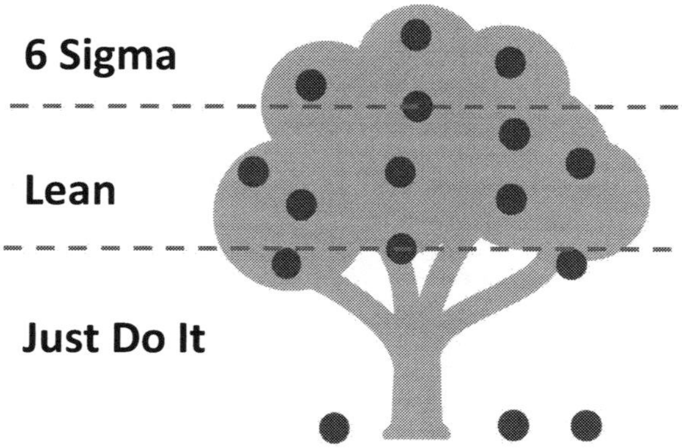

Figure 6.11 – Bearing the Fruits of Process Improvement

Ideally, process improvement should seek to optimize the process in terms of its effectiveness and efficiency.

Value-stream mapping, a Lean technique, can be utilized to analyze the current state and design the future state of an end-to-end process for delivering a product or service to customers. This method identifies and eliminates non-value-added activities, or 'waste,' wherever possible.

Waste is defined as any activities or outcomes that does not add value to the customer. In the workplace, there are typically 8 types of waste recognized, often remembered by the acronym DOWNTIME, hence depicting the first letter of each waste:

1. Defects: Products or services that fail to meet quality standards and necessitate rework or correction.
2. Overproduction: Producing more than what is needed or before it is needed, leading to excess inventory and storage costs.
3. Waiting: Delays or idle time when people, materials, or equipment are not actively working or being processed.
4. Non-utilized Talent: Not effectively utilizing the skills, creativity, or knowledge of employees.
5. Transportation: Unnecessary movement or handling of materials or products within the supply chain or production process.
6. Inventory: Excess raw materials, work-in-progress (WIP), or finished goods that tie up capital and space without adding immediate value.

7. Motion: Unnecessary movements by people or equipment that do not contribute to the production process.
8. Excess Processing: Doing more work than is required to meet customer requirements, such as over-engineering or using overly complex processes.

As the processes are improved, they need to be standardized, i.e., documented and adhered to … *'do it right'* and *'make it stick'*.

Processes are documented with procedures and work instructions. A procedure is normally in the form of a swimlane flowchart diagram, as shown in Figure 6.12, outlining the steps that are to be followed by each role. Work instructions provide details on how to execute the steps within the swimlanes. All steps within a swimlane do not necessarily require a work instruction.

As previously stated, we are not standardizing for the sake of standardizing. Standardizing is about capturing and maintaining the gains of process improvement, i.e., no back sliding.

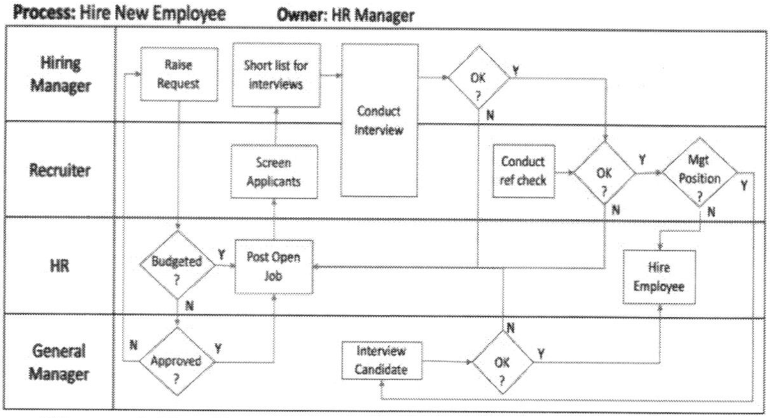

Figure 6.12 – Example of procedure in form of swimlane

Process Mining

For business processes enabled by software applications, process mining has received increasing attention as an approach to better understand current ‘as-is’ state in order to expose improvement opportunities. In essence, process mining involves analyzing the event logs maintained by software applications to reveal the true process that is being executed. Process mining is done using specialized software applications, which captures data from transaction systems and provides detailed information about how business processes are performing. It can help identify where there may be opportunities to automate using software ‘robots’, known as Robotic Process Automation (RPA), which is an emerging technology designed to automate the repetitive, high-volume-but-low-value tasks employees are doing on their desktops.

Kaizen Blitz

A Kaizen Blitz, also referred to as rapid improvement workshop, is a focused, short-term event, normally between 2 and 5 days to improve a business process. It is an event by which the participants can learn new concepts and approaches, and then put them into practice.

Figure 6.13 Kaizen Blitz

Kaizen Blitz has four significant advantages, namely: it's fast, it increases learning retention, creates ownership, and promotes teamwork. It is not intended to deliver a nicely polished solution but rather a strawman which can then be refined over time. It increases the retention of the new learnings because it is generally recognized that people better learn by doing as illustrated in Figure 6.14.

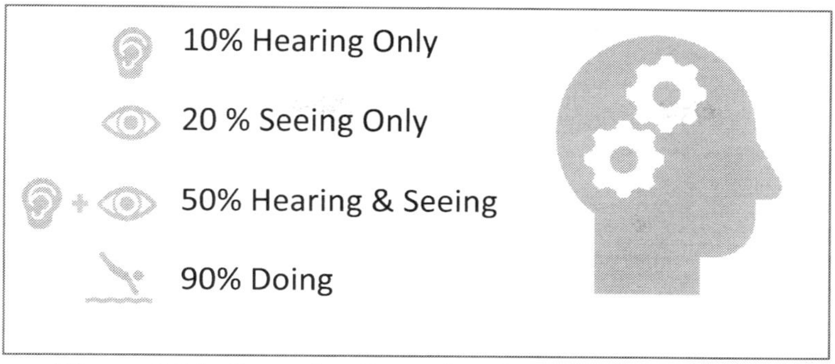

Figure 6.14 - Learning Retention (recall after 72 hours)

To execute a Kaizen Blitz, it involves four steps as shown in Figure 6.15, and further explained below.

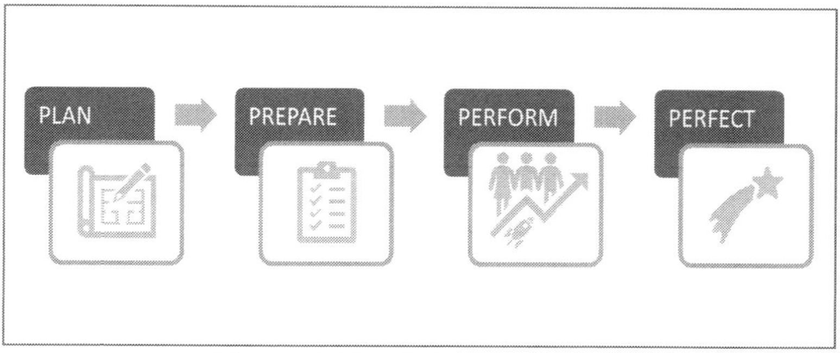

Figure 6.15 – Kaizen Blitz Steps

1. Plan:
    a. Define the goal, scope, and deliverables.
    b. Designate experienced facilitator.
    c. Set budget for team's discretionary spend if applicable.
    d. Set the agenda:
        i. Normally 2 to 5 days
        ii. Learn-then-do approach
        iii. Report out every end of day
    e. Set rules of engagement (example in Figure 6.16)

    f. Determine who will participate:
        i. Fully dedicated
        ii. Normally between 5 to 30 participants
        iii. Organize in sub-group for larger events (example in Figure 6.17)
    g. Build Pert chart of activities (example in Figure 6.18).
2. Prepare:
    a. Order required materials and equipment.
    b. Book required room(s).
    c. Schedule interruption in normal operations.
    d. Make key stakeholder aware.
    e. Baseline performance indicators.
    f. Conduct analysis / fact finding / pre-design.
    g. Prepare educational material.
    h. Brief participants
3. Perform:
    a. Review agenda and rules of engagement.
    b. Execute Pert chart activities.
    c. Report progress daily to key stakeholders. (example in Figure 6.19)
    d. Set post-kaizen plan, goals and objectives.
4. Perfect:
    a. Execute post-kaizen plan through Project Management.
    b. Apply Progress Management to drive continuous improvement.
    c. Normally 3 to 6 months after Kaizen, verify if desired results have been achieved.

- Be punctual, present and active
- Challenge status quo... ask Why 5 times
- Attack the problem and not the person
- Be open minded... compromise if necessary to achieve consensus
- Don't let perfection get in way of progress... have a bias for action
- Seek quick and simple low-cost solutions
- There are no failures only learnings

Figure 6.16 – Kaizen Blitz Rules of Engagement

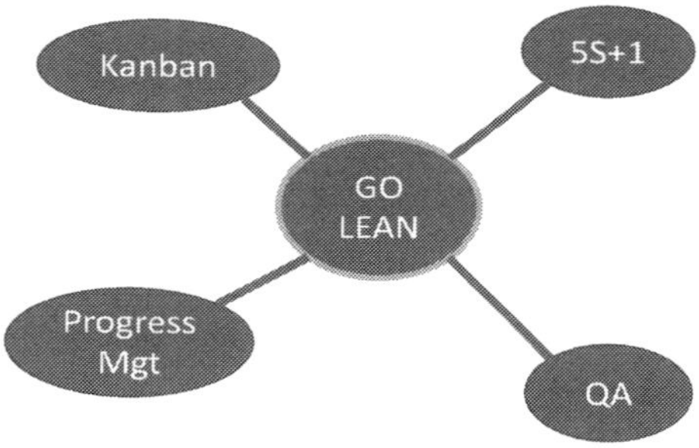

Figure 6.17 – Kaizen Blitz teams

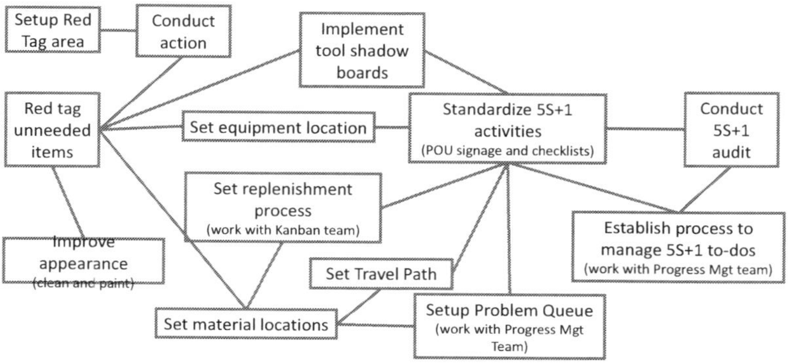

Figure 6.18 - Example of Pert Chart of Activities (5S Team)

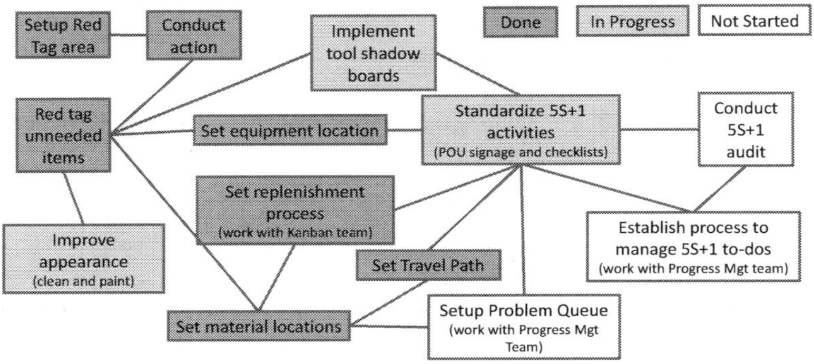

Figure 6.19 – Example of how pert chart can be used to report progress.

Data Governance

An essential factor to keep in mind when establishing operational policies and procedures is acknowledging that data serves as the lifeblood of any business process. Data encompasses all the raw facts, figures, and statistics that are collected, stored, and processed within an organization. Data is integral to every aspect of a business process, from its inception to its execution and ongoing optimization. It enables organizations to make informed decisions, drive efficiency, and ultimately achieve their goals.

Data has proven to be a very valuable asset for organizations who properly manage and leverage data to protect, improve and grow their business.

"Data is the new oil. Like oil, data is valuable, but if unrefined it cannot really be used. Oil has to be changed into gas, plastic, chemicals, etc. to create a valuable entity that drives profitable activity; so, data must be broken down and analyzed for it to have value." [12]

Therefore, proper data governance needs to be in place to ensure the overall management of the availability, usability, integrity, and security of data used within an organization. It needs to encompass the people, processes, and technologies required to ensure that data assets are managed effectively throughout the data lifecycle.

To be effective, data governance must be integrated into business process management, including the following key components:

1. Data Policies and Standards: Defining how data shall be managed, including data quality standards, privacy policies, and data security protocols.
2. Data Stewardship: Assigning responsibility to specific individuals or teams within the organization who act as data stewards, ensuring that data is managed according to established policies and standards.
3. Data Quality Management: Implementing processes and technologies to monitor and improve the quality of data, including data cleansing, validation, and data quality metrics.
4. Data Security and Privacy: Implementing measures to protect data from unauthorized access, loss, or corruption, as well as ensuring compliance with relevant data privacy regulations.
5. Data Lifecycle Management: Managing data throughout its lifecycle, from creation and ingestion to archival or deletion, including processes for data retention and disposal.

6. Data Governance Framework: Developing a comprehensive framework that outlines the structure, processes, and responsibilities for data governance within the organization.
7. Data Governance Tools: Utilizing software tools and platforms to support data governance activities, such as data cataloging, metadata management, and data lineage tracking.

Chapter Summary / Key Takeaways

Process management entails optimizing and standardizing business processes to align with strategic objectives.

It begins with modeling the organization's business processes, assigning clear ownership, and establishing operational policies.

Key performance indicators are then utilized to assess process efficiency and effectiveness, facilitating management and the identification of improvement opportunities. Priority is given to processes with significant strategic impact for improvement initiatives.

Often, mapping the existing process reveals straightforward improvements, termed "low hanging fruits," which can be swiftly implemented ("*just do it*").

Subsequently, Lean-Six-Sigma methodologies are employed to garner additional improvements, with Kaizen Blitz serving as an effective execution tool for these improvements.

As the processes are improved, they need to be standardized, i.e., documented and adhered to … *'do it right'* and *'make it stick'*.

An essential factor to keep in mind when establishing operational policies and procedures is acknowledging that data serves as the lifeblood of any business process.

CHAPTER 7

Performance Management

Performance Management is the heart of CIMS because it is what truly makes it all happen, … People.

It involves creating a work environment in which employees are encouraged and enabled to grow and perform to the best of their abilities.

The organization's performance is a function of the employees' motivation, their ability, and the environment wherein they work, all which can be expressed as a formula as shown in Figure 7.1.

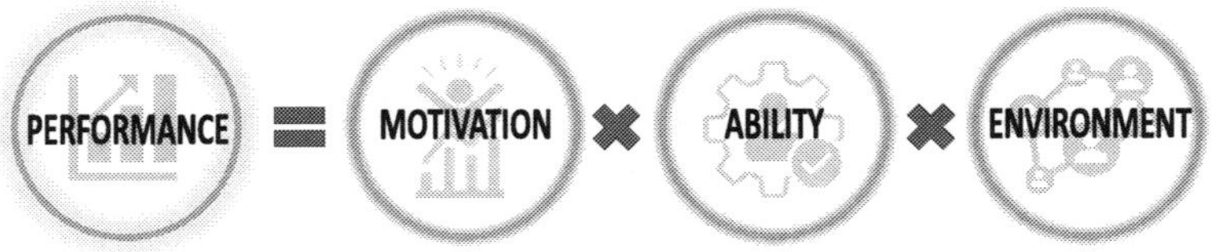

Figure 7.1 – Performance Equation

Motivation

Being motivated, means that a person is giving his/her best. They are trying hard to get the job done. Motivated employees in the workplace means that they are highly engaged to the success of the organization. Continuous improvement cannot truly happen without having an engaged workforce.

Organizations that foster high employee engagement are likely to excel in customer satisfaction and achieve high levels of productivity, operational efficiency, and profitability. Additionally, they often experience safer, healthier employees with lower absenteeism and reduced turnover.

So, what is the best way to motivate employees, i.e., increase their engagement levels?

Probably the most popular theory of motivation is Maslow's hierarchies of needs, which asserts that individuals' most basic needs must first be met before they become motivated to achieve higher level needs. Basically, Maslow's Hierarchy of needs is a pyramid of different levels of needs as illustrated in Figure 7.2. Only after fulfilling lower-level needs like physiological and safety can employees achieve higher levels such as esteem and self-actualization, leading to increased efficiency, motivation, and innovative thinking

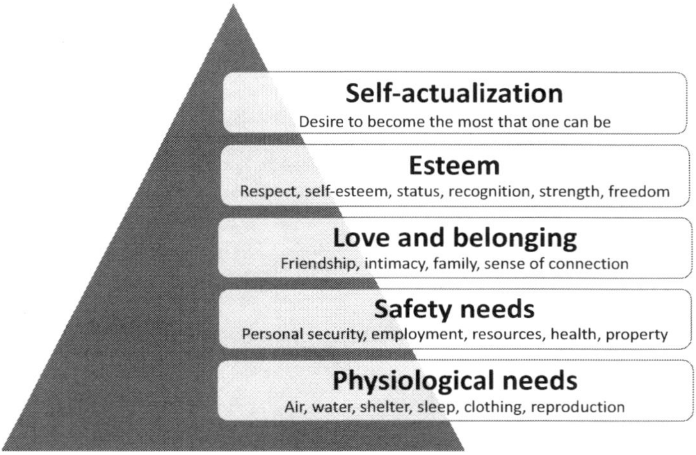

Figure 7.2 – Maslow's Hierarchy of Needs

The organization must therefore endeavor to ensure that employees are satisfied in lower-level needs by compensating them competitively as well as providing a reasonable level of job security and a safe and respectful working environment.

Participative leadership applied properly can help create a spirit and sense of belonging. Involving employees in decision making and process improvement normally builds up their confidence so that they can satisfy their higher needs in esteem and self-actualization. This, in fact, creates a reinforcing loop in as much that employees who are given the opportunity to innovate normally become more engaged, and more engaged employees will tend to be more innovative.

Ability

Ability is synonymous with capability, potential, or capacity. It determines whether one possesses the means to do something.

In the context of CIMS, ability is not just about being able to do a job per se. It requires a combination of hard and soft skills. Hard skills are technical skills and knowledge to do the job. Whereas soft skills relate to ability to:

- Learn and grow
- Be agile and collaborative
- Identify improvement opportunities
- Solve problems and improve processes

To enable continuous improvement, there should be a number of employees certified in Lean and Six Sigma. This certification comes in various skill levels: Yellow Belt, Green Belt, Black Belt, and Master Black Belt. These certifications can be obtained through a number of accreditations such as IASSC (The International Association for Six Sigma Certification) [13] or ASQ (American Society for Quality). [14]

Moreover, all employees should get basic training on the applicable concepts and be able to recognize waste in the workplace as discussed in the previous charter (i.e., DOWNTIME).

Another important aspect to the employee's ability is to become multi-skilled and able to move up and down the line to where the work needs to be accomplished. Figure 7.3 illustrates the advantages of having multi-skilled vs. single-skilled employees. It shows two scenarios of three jobs that are executed sequentially, one with single-skilled employees and the other with multi-skilled employees. The output with the single-skilled employees is limited to the pacing job, hence job A, which is 2 units per hours. Whereas, with multiskilled employees, the employee at job B can also perform job A, resulting in achieving an average output of 3 units per hour, which in this example is a 50% productivity improvement over having single-skilled employees.

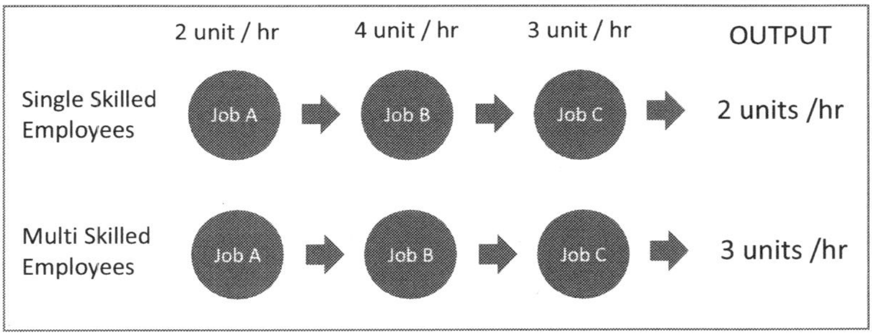

Figure 7.3 – Single vs. multiskilled employees

Environment

Employees may be motivated and able, but to perform well they also need a work environment that supports and empowers them to perform. The proper environment will reinforce their motivation, whereas a poor one will erode it.

I believe that an environment conducive to continuous improvement has to be on the '*TROT*'… there has to be **T**rust, **R**espect, **O**penness and **T**eamwork.

Trust is really the foundation. Participative leadership cannot really be effective without it.

A highly recommended book is "The Speed of Trust: The One Thing that Changes Everything" by Stephen M.R. Covey. In it, he explores how trust, and the speed at which it is built with clients, employees, and constituents, is crucial for creating a high-performance, successful organization. “Over time, I have come to this simple definition of leadership: Leadership is getting results in a way that inspires trust.” [15]

It really falls on the leadership to create the right environment to make continuous improvement a way of life. The CIMS framework will not make it happen without a leadership that is passionate, persistent, and present.

Means & Media

Performance Management is often seen as the process to manage the performance of employees, such as setting goals, coaching, and evaluating employees. However, in the context of CIMS, it needs to encompass the organization as a whole. Performance Management needs to ensure proper alignment to the organization’s strategic goals. Figure 7.4 illustrates some of the means by which this can be achieved with the media that can be used to enable it and covered in more detail below.

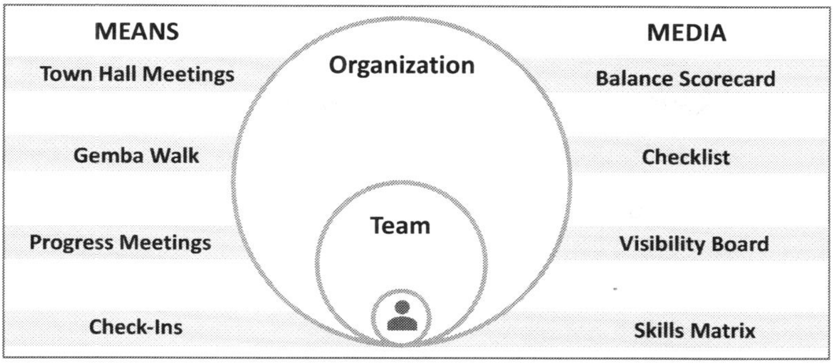

Figure 7.4 – Performance Management Means and Media

Town Hall Meetings

Town hall meetings, also referred to as 'town halls', are organization-wide meetings in which the top management communicates goals and reports progress as well as address employees' questions and concerns. It is also an opportunity to recognize and celebrates wins.

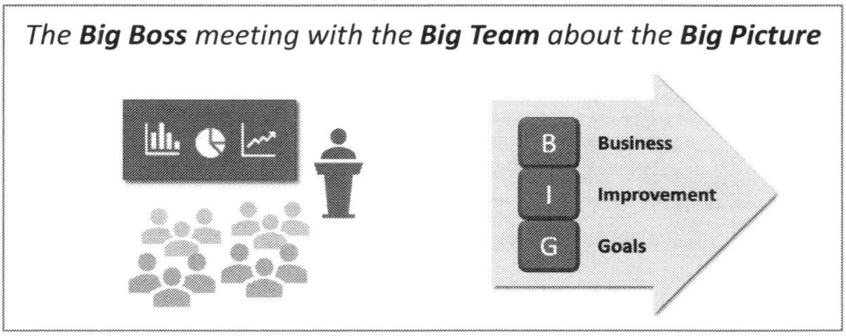

Figure 7.5 – Town Hall Meeting

Town halls should be held quarterly or, at the very least, annually. Depending on the size of the organization, they may be held in the cafeteria or offsite at a hotel or convention center and/or virtually.

I strongly believe that town hall meetings are important because employees want and need to hear from the 'big boss' and understand the 'big picture', able to connect the dots between their goals and objectives to the organization's strategic goals. The balance scorecard is a good communication tool to summarize how well the organization is doing. As illustrated in Figure 7.6, it can be shown with traffic light indicators to highlight the performance to date. This would be coupled with showing trend charts and providing more details for each of the key performance indicators.

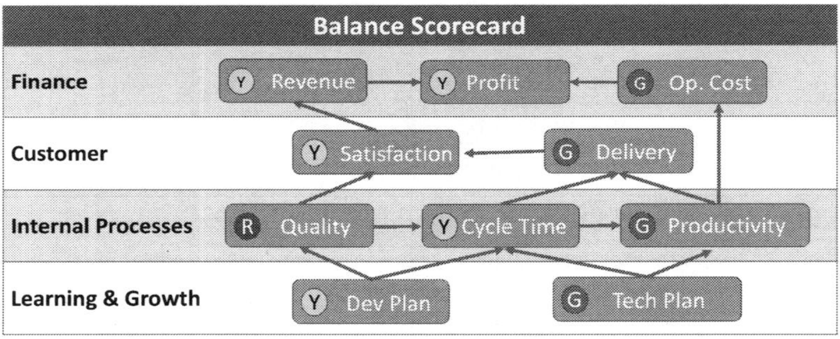

Figure 7.6 – Balance Scorecard using traffic light indicators to summarize performance.

From my experience, town hall meetings can be challenging. Your message may not always be good news and you may face confrontational questions or comments. There may be some 'wildcard' questions that you would have never anticipated. I've had situations, where the union executives used this forum to drive their agenda and challenge management's integrity. It is therefore important to anticipate and be prepared to answer difficult questions. In answering tough questions, my only advise is that the leader needs to speak with compassion, genuineness, and honesty – because truth builds trust.

Gemba Walks

In the context of CIMS, participative leadership is not just about involving employees, but it is also about leaders themselves being significantly visible and involved. The leaders must help remove barriers as well as coach and guide the team.

Leaders cannot just '*talk the talk*', they must also '*walk the walk*'.

A very effective way to achieve this is by conducting what is referred to as "Gemba Walks", which was made popular by Toyota. The term "gemba" means "the real place" in Japanese. For process improvement, "gemba" is the place where the real work happens. A Gemba Walk is similar to what is commonly known as "Management by Walking Around (MBWA)" but with a more disciplined approach. The steps to follow are summarized in Figure 7.7. In essence, it involves picking a theme against which the leader will conduct a process check and prepare a checklist of the questions that need to be answered. The leader then walks the process to observe and collect the required information. This may involve a number of brief walks (1/2 to 1 hours) for several days and at different times during the day. In doing the walks, the leader may ask questions but should not critique or make suggestions during his/her observations. Only after should the leader share with the team his/her observations and suggestions for potential improvement opportunities.

In the same spirit, it is good for senior leaders to attend Progress meetings to witness their effectiveness at the various levels of the organization and again identify opportunities for improvement.

1. Pick a theme (e.g., cycle time, safety, etc.)
2. Prepare a checklist
3. Go where it happens
4. Focus on process not people
5. Record your observations. Don't make suggestions during the walk
6. Follow-up... share with the team what you have seen and learned

Figure 7.7 – Steps to conducting a Gemba Walk

Progress Management

Progress and Performance Management are integral to each other. One could say that Progress Management is really the performance management process of the teams. It involves making the team's performance visible in the workplace and engaging employees in continuously seeking improvements. Performance Management involves ensuring alignment to the organization's strategic goals. Each employee's goals and objectives, including their development plan need to satisfy the need of their team, which in turn needs to be aligned to the strategic goals of the organization.

Check-Ins

Many organizations are doing away with formal performance reviews. Research cited by the Society for

Human Resource Management [16] reveals that nearly all managers (95%) are dissatisfied with formal performance appraisals, and most HR professionals (90%) think the appraisals are inaccurate. Many employees don't like them either. Employee complaints about performance appraisals are that the reviews do not reward high performers or deal with poor performers and are disrespectful and untimely. Fewer employers gave formal performance ratings: 80% in 2017 compared to 85% in 2016. But more reported frequent—at least quarterly—informal performance check-ins.

I have experienced the transition from an appraisal system to check-ins and believe that there is merit to this shift. The conversation does not get bogged down to the rating. It is more of an open dialogue about the employee's progress relative to previously agreed-to goals and development objectives, both in terms of satisfying the needs of the organization and the employee's career aspiration.

Skills Matrix

As previously stated, another important aspect to the employee's ability is to become multi-skilled, which results in having a more agile and productive team. An effective tool to manage training is the skills matrix as illustrated in Figure 7.8, which should be posted on the team's visibility board. You will note that it includes process improvement skills as well as planned training.

The skills matrix promptly identifies deficiencies that may impede team functionality, potentially leading to bottlenecks where only one individual can carry out tasks. Worse still, if this sole individual handles a critical function and departs or becomes unavailable for any reason, a crisis may ensue. These instances are commonly known as 'single points of failure'.

Machine Shop Skills & Training

○ Planned
◔ Training
◑ Can do with help
◕ Can do solo
● Can train others

	Planning	NC Program	Saw	Mill	Lather	Router	Process	Paint	Assembly	QA	5S	Kaizen	Safety	6 Six Sigma	Progress Report
Diane D.	●	◕								◕	◕	◕	◕	●	◕
Gabrielle C.	◑	○								◔	◑	◑	◕	○	◔
JR C.		●	◕	◕	◕	◕	○	○	◕	●	●	●	◕	●	●
Marc R.		◕	◑	◑	◑	◑	◑		◑	◕	◕	◕	◕	◑	●
Sue B.	●									◕	●	●	●	◕	●
Francois G.			●	●	●	●	◕	◕	◕	●	◕	◕	◕	○	●
Yves L.			◕	●	●	◑			◑		◕	◔	◕		
Andre B.	●	●		○	○	○					●	●	◕	●	●
Leo C.							●	●	◔	◔	◔	◔	◕		
Richard D.							◑	◑	●	◔	◑	◑	◕		○

Figure 7.8 – Skills Matrix

Chapter Summary / Key Takeaways

At the heart of CIMS, Performance Management involves creating a work environment in which employees are encouraged and enabled to grow and perform to the best of their abilities.

The organization's performance is a function of the employees' motivation, their ability, and the environment in which they work. Therefore, Performance Management must address these three variables.

Motivated employees in the workplace means that they are highly engaged to the success of the organization. An environment conducive to continuous improvement must be on the '*TROT*' that is there has to be **T**rust, **R**espect, **O**penness and **T**eamwork.

Participate Leadership can have a significant impact on the level of employee engagement. Leaders need to 'talk the talk' and more importantly 'walk the walk'. On a regular basis there should be town hall meetings where the 'big boss' meets with the 'big team' about the 'big picture'.

Leaders must be actively visible and involved in continuous improvement. An effective approach is to have senior leaders do what is known as "Gemba Walks", which has them going to real place where work is performed and observing to identify improvement opportunities, which is afterwards shared with the team during their Progress meetings.

Moreover, regular check-ins, one-on-one meetings, should be held between each employee and his/her manager to review progress against the employee's performance and development objectives as well as establish the best path forward to his/her continued growth.

CHAPTER 8

Making it Happen

First and foremost, there needs to be commitment from the top to properly implement and maintain CIMS.

'Talking the talk' is easy, but 'walking the walk' may be more difficult for a lot of leaders who have grown and have been successful in chaotic organizations without any formal management system. These leaders are often where they are because they prove to be great 'firefighters', able to manage through crisis. Transitioning to CIMS for these leaders may be very difficult, because they will not get the immediate reward that they get from putting out fires. They will no longer get the rush of a crisis and a sense of accomplishment in having heroically solved a crisis. These leaders tend to also be more autocratic in their leadership style because when there is a 'fire', there is no time to discuss and seek input and consensus. Also, in putting out 'fires' they will tend to not deal with the root cause but only suppress the symptoms by patching the problem.

Dr. Deming put it well: "One gets a good rating for fighting a fire. The result is visible; can be quantified. If you do it right the first time, you are invisible. You satisfied the requirements. That is your job. Mess it up, and correct it later, you become a hero." [9]

Figure 8.1 illustrates conceptually the change in the leadership's focus when moving from a firefighting organization to a continuous improvement organization. Their focus changes from mainly dealing with problems to developing their employees and improving the business processes, which results in the volume of problems diminishing over time.

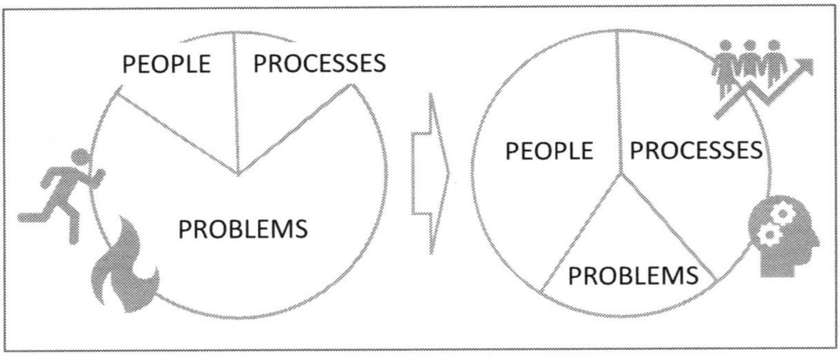

Figure 8.1 –Leadership shift in focus from firefighting to CIMS

An article published in the Harvard Business Review entitled "Stop Fire Fighting" [17] made the following observations: "There are some companies that never fight fires, even though they have just as much work and just as many resource constraints as companies that do. How do they avoid firefighting? The short answer is that they have strong problem-solving cultures. They don't tackle a problem unless they're committed to understanding its root cause and finding a valid solution. They perform triage. They set realistic deadlines. Perhaps most important, they don't reward firefighting."

For leaders to fundamentally change their ways, there will need to be *Significant Emotion Events (SEE*s), which can either be negative or positive, or as they say in layman terms: *Oh-shit* or *Aha* moments.

Negative *SEE*s may be as a result of losing business or not being able to make improvements stick. It may also come as result of *'tough love'* from shareholders... "*Be Good or Be Gone*" as the Irish folk song by Fionn Regan goes.

Positive *SEE*s may come from new learnings or experiences which result in the leader aspiring to the potential gains that may be achieved by adopting better ways. Probably the most impactfully, although not always possible, is to have the senior leadership team go on a field trip and visit world class companies.

As briefly discussed in chapter one, this is how Boeing got their senior leaders to SEE. In the late 1980's, senior executives went on what they referred to as the "Japan Study Missions". To say the least, it was an eye opener. Bruce Gissing, one of the Boeing executives, stated: "The bottom line is that the team came back shocked. Our arrogant belief that we were high-productivity producers was shattered". Another interesting comment "Thank God Toyota is not in the aerospace industry!". [4]

Another approach, albeit not as exciting, is to buy benchmarking services, such as those provided by the American Productivity & Quality Center (APQC), which positions itself as the world's foremost authority in benchmarking, best practices, process and performance improvement, and knowledge management. [11]

CIMS Maturity Model

The extent of change required by CIMS will vary based on the organization's current maturity level, which can be evaluated using the maturity model depicted in Figure 8.2 and further detailed in Figure 8.3.

In enhance, each level can be summarized as follows:

Level 1 – Ad-hoc: The organization is very informal. Little is documented in terms of strategies, goals, and operating policies. The business mostly runs on tribal knowledge. The organization doesn't really know where it is going.

Level 2 – Directional: The organization has set and shared its vision, strategies, and goals… it knows where it is going.

Level 3 – Actionable: Same as level 2 plus executable plans are in place to achieve the goals. Opportunities for improvement are being captured and actions are being deployed. The organization is positioned to '*get it done*'.

Level 4 – Optimal: Same as level 3 plus leading practices and methodologies are being applied to '*do it right*'.

Level 5 – Motivational: Same as level 4 plus leadership is highly visible and actively involved coupled with high employee engagement to '*make it stick*'.

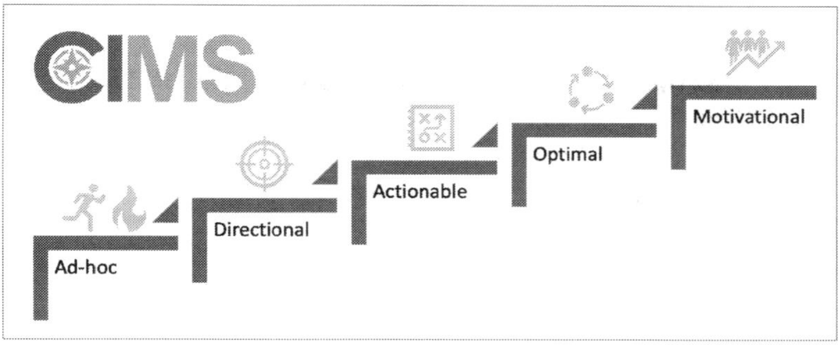

Figure 8.2 – CIMS maturity model

CIMS	1 Ad-hoc ☹	2 Directional 😕
Plan	Business planning is mostly unstructured. Plans are siloed, uncoordinated across organization. Org tends to be reactive.	The organization's vision and strategic goals (3 to 5 years) and initiatives have been set.
Progress	Progress to the plan is monitored by management but not as a team. Team meetings are seldom.	Regular team meetings are held to review performance and deploy action as required.
Process	No operating policies. Processes are mostly not standardized or measured. Business running on tribal knowledge and heroics.	Process classification framework in place with clear process ownership. Operating Policies for all tier 1 processes are defined.
Project	Projects are managed in an ad hoc way. No proper governance and controls. Low Project success rate.	Project are formally chartered (objectives, scope, deliverables, time, $, assumptions, team members, and sponsoring body).
Performance	Scarce or no performance feedback. Or difficult to link individual expectations to organizational goals. Low employee engagement.	Performance expectations are communicated and are aligned to organizational goals.

Figure 8.3 – CIMS Maturity Model (1/2)

3 Actionable	4 Optimal	5 Motivational
L2 + Integrated business planning (IBP) is in place to balance supply and demand, including the execution and impact of strategic initiatives.	L3 + The goals are set from a balance perspective, and strategic initiatives are established using a system thinking approach.	L4 + High sense of commitment and urgency to the plan. Catch-ball actively being used to negotiate objectives and plans.
L2 + Progress to the plan is visible in the workplace. Opportunities for improvement are captured and being actioned.	L3 + PDCA cycles are at a proper cadence for each team allowing for timely adjustments and improvements. Getting to root causes 'Ask Why 5 Times'	L4 + 'Stop the line' concept is in place with management actively involved in helping remove blockers.
L2 + Processes are measured for their effectiveness and efficiency, and improvements opportunities are identified and being actioned.	L3 + Lean-Six-Sigma is being applied to improve and standardize processes that have the greatest impact on organizational goals.	L4 + Continuous cycle to standardize, stabilize and improve processes using a Kaizen Blitz approach with high employee involvement.
L2 + Proper project planning and controls are in place (Gantt, budget, issues, risks, etc). *'Get it Done'*	L3 + Stage Gating is used to validate path forward. Proper methodologies are applied (e.g., Waterfall, Agile, SDLC, Lean Six-Sigma). *'Do it Right'*	L4 + Change Management is integrated in whole approach. High Project Success Rate. *'Make it Stick'*
L2 + Regular 1 on 1 Check-Ins are conducted to discuss progress and best path forward for growth and development. Team training matrix are used and visible in the work area.	L3 + Leadership frequently conducts Gemba Walks and holds team meetings to review and encourage performance.	L4 + Town Hall meetings held at least yearly to reinforce alignment to org goals. Employee can clearly see the 'golden thread' of their performance objectives to the organization's goals.

Figure 8.3 – CIMS Maturity Model (2/2)

Takeoff

Following the successful implementation of the "World Class" management system at Boeing Canada's Arnprior division, I was tasked with supporting our sister division in Winnipeg to adopt the same approach. Drawing from my experience with kaizen blitz over the previous two years, I believed it would provide an effective launchpad for Winnipeg's initiative. This approach yielded significant success and in many other occasions since.

A kaizen blitz for CIMS' takeoff is a one-week event involving the senior management team and key players representing middle and front-line management as well as staff.

A sample agenda is shown in Figure 8.5. In essence, it starts with Plan Management by conducting a strategic planning session (as explained in chapter 3) and closes with Project Management in setting a task list to complete the implementation of CIMS.

At first glance, this may seem straight forward. However, there is a lot to cover in one week and it can be easily spoiled by lack of preparation, poor facilitation, or unengaged leadership.

A detailed agenda needs to be established with the topics to be covered, the time allotted and the owner for each. The owners are responsible to prepare for their assigned topics, which would normally involve preparing and delivering a presentation or leading an exercise.

To successfully conduct such a kaizen, an experienced and unbiased facilitator is essential. The role of the facilitator is to keep the group focused, guide in applying proper approach, and hold true to the rules of engagement as outlined in Figure 8.4. It would be advisable to post the rules in the room where the kaizen is being held.

1. **Be prepared**... do your homework
2. **Be punctual and present**... unplug your devices
3. **Be open and respectful**... listen, do not interrupt
4. **Be engaged**... argue your points... Silence is Approval
5. **Be candid**... attack the problem, not the person
6. **Be compromising** to seek consensus

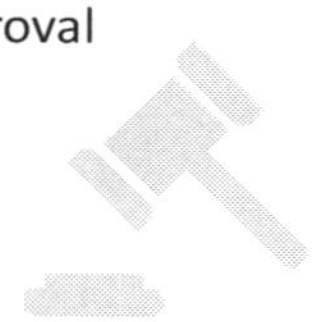

Figure 8.4 – CIMS Kaizen Rules of Engagement

TIME	MONDAY	TUESDAY	WEDNESDAY	THURSDAY	FRIDAY
8:00	**CIMS Overview**	4. How we overcome barriers?	Integrated Business Planning	**PROGRESS MANAGEMENT**	Gamba Walk Report Out
8:30	Current maturity level	Brainstorm		Set Check/Act Calendar	
9:00	**PLAN MANAGEMENT**				
9:30	1. Where do we stand today?	Affinitize			**PROJECT MANAGEMENT**
10:00	Mission / KPIs		**PROCESS MANAGEMENT**	How will we execute?	Set CIMS Maturity Targets
10:30		Prioritize	1. Set standards		Set Plan to make it happen
11:00	SWOT		2. Model the business	Where "stop the line" applies?	Brainstorm
11:30	2. Where do we want to be?		3. Assign Ownership		
12:00	Lunch	Lunch	Lunch	Lunch	Lunch
12:30	Vision & Strategic Goals	5. Who needs to do what?	4&5 Tier 1 KPIs & Policies	**PERFORMANCE MANAGEMENT**	Affinitize
13:00		Tier 1 X-Matrix		Build Balance Scorecard	
13:30	3. What are the barriers?				Pert Chart
14:00	Brainstorm	Tier 2 X-Matrices	6. Select tier 2 processes		
14:30				Gamba Walk	Buffer time
15:00	Affinitize			Prep checklist	
15:30				Perform	
16:00	Rationalize				
16:30					
17:00	Process Check	Process Check	Process Check	Process Check	Process Check

Figure 8.5 – CIMS Kaizen Blitz Agenda

CIMO

Many organizations have seen the benefits of having a Project Management Office (PMO) in order to provide governance, oversight and support to the successful delivery of projects.

In the same spirit, I am proposing that the mandate of the PMO be broadened to become a Continuous Improvement Management Office (CIMO). To be clear, I am not suggesting that process improvement be centralized and executed by a specific group. At the contrary, to make continuous improvement a way of life, it needs to be imbedded in the daily activities throughout the organization. CIMO instead would have the mandate to build competencies, methods, processes, and in-house standards as well as provide coaching and support. CIMS, in itself, needs to be standardized and optimized, and continuously improved.

CIMO should be a relatively small group of experienced specialists, such as certified project and change managers as well as Lean Six Sigma Blackbelts.

The following outlines how the CIMO can support and reinforce CIMS:

1. Plan Management
    a. Organize and facilitate strategic planning sessions.
    b. Coordinate benchmarking activities.
    c. Maintain and publish the organization's Vision, Mission, Values, and Goals.
    d. Coordinate Integrated Business Planning.

2. Project Management
    a. Standardize and improve project management processes, methodologies and tools.
    b. Provide training, coaching and support.
    c. Maintain repository of lessons learned.
    d. Conduct project health checks and stage gate reviews.
    e. Track and report progress of projects.
    f. Help redress projects in trouble.
3. Progress Management
    a. Set standards for visibility boards, dashboards, metrics, skills matrix, etc.
    b. Provide training, coaching and support.
    c. Maintain and publish calendar of Progress meetings across the organization.
    d. Conduct process checks / audits.
4. Process Management
    a. Establish process management standards and maturity model.
    b. Provide training, coaching and support.
    c. Administer process classification framework.
    d. Help process owners keep abreast of industry best practices.
    e. Maintain repository of all policies and procedures.
    f. Provide visibility of the progress in increasing the maturity level of the processes.

g. Conduct audits to ensure compliance to policies, procedures and work instructions.
h. Coordinate activities to support external audits, e.g., ISO certification.

5. Performance Management
    a. Establish and execute internal branding plan.
    b. Deliver soft skills training.
    c. Organize town hall meetings.
    d. Conduct or coordinate employee engagement surveys.
    e. Conduct process check / audits of employee check-ins.
    f. Monitor and report progress of employee development.

STOP, ... and Think!

As the organization moves forward on its journey of continuous improvement, it will come to crossroads where choices will have to be made. There will be problematic or opportunistic situations for which several options exist to solve or exploit these situations. It is therefore important that the leadership make informed and measured decisions in order to select the optimal solution.

A very effective method to analyze options and present proposals to senior management is using the STOP method, which involves outlining the Situation, Target, Options and Proposal.

This is an approach derived from a problem-solving technique I learned when at Boeing referred to as "STP", which stands for Situation-Target-Proposal. I simply added "O" so that the potential options would also be clearly articulated and evaluated.

In essence it involves presenting the following:

- Situation: describe the problem /opportunity, hence the current state. This can be a combination of facts, data, graphs, diagrams, beliefs, and opinions. It could even simply be the results of the 5-Why technique discussed in chapter 5.
- Target: specify the desired outcome, hence the future state. This may be in the form of a vision, expectations, goals, and/or objectives.
- Options: First present the potential options that could close the gaps between the current and future states. And then evaluate these options against the stated targets as illustrated in Figure 8.6.
- Proposal: And finally recommend the preferred option and next steps.

TARGETS	Option 1	Option 2	Option 3
QUALITY	Does not fully meet requirements		
TIME		Extends timeline by 1 month	
COST		$500k above budget	$100k above budget
RISK	Small vendor		Complexity

Figure 8.6 – Analysis of Options vs Targets

I have found that using the STOP method as the standard approach by which proposals are presented to senior management has greatly helped accelerate the decision-making process. In fact, when a STOP is well done, acceptance of the proposal becomes a no-brainer.

Chapter Summary / Key Takeaways

To make it happen, there needs to be, first and foremost, commitment from the top. This is an absolute prerequisite. For leaders who have grown in firefighting organizations, it will be very difficult for them to change and accept a more structured and proactive approach as well as adopt a participative leadership style. For these leaders to change there will need to be a *Significant Emotional Event* (*SEE*)… 'Aha' or 'Oh Shit' moments.

Once commitment is attained, then the most effective approach for CIMS to 'take off' is to conduct a kaizen blitz involving the senior management team and key players representing middle and front-line management as well as staff. This is only the start of a journey requiring constant nourishment and reinforcement, which I would suggest warrants having a Continuous Improvement Management Office (CIMO).

As the organization moves forward, it will come to crossroads where choices will need to be made. The *STOP* method is an effective way to establish the best path forward, hence articulating the Situation, Target, Options and Proposal.

Bibliography

[1] T. F. Wallace, MRPII: Making It Happen, New York: Oliver Wight, 1985.

[2] W. A. Sandras, Just-in-Time: Making It Happen: Unleashing the Power of Continuous Improvement, Wiley, 1989.

[3] J. Black, A World-Class Production System, Crisp Publications, 1998.

[4] J. Black, Lean Production, Implementing a World Class System, Industrial Press, Inc., 2008.

[5] R. S. &. N. D. P. Kaplan, "The Balanced Scorecard: Measures That Drive Performance.," *Harvard Business Review,* 1992.

[6] S. Buehring, "Knowledge Train: PRINCE2® vs the PMBOK® Guide: A comparison," 29 March 2019. [Online]. Available: https://www.knowledgetrain.co.uk/resources/qualifications/prince2-and-pmbok-guide-comparison. [Accessed April 2019].

[7] J. P. Kotter, Leading Change, Boston: Harvard Business Review Press, 1996.

[8] J. Hiatt, "PROSCI," [Online]. Available: https://www.prosci.com/adkar. [Accessed April 2019].

[9] E. W. Demings, Out of Crisis, Cambridge, Mass.: MIT , 1986.

[10] "ABPMP Association of Business Process Management Professionals," [Online]. Available: https://www.abpmp.org. [Accessed Febuary 2019].

[11] "APQC (American Productivity & Quality Center)," [Online]. Available: https://www.apqc.org/about. [Accessed March 2019].

[12] W. contributors, "Clive Humby," 29 January 2024. [Online]. Available: https://en.wikipedia.org/w/index.php?title=Clive_Humby&oldid=1200386127.

[13] "International Association for Six Sigma Certification," [Online]. Available: https://www.iassc.org. [Accessed April 2019].

[14] "American Society for Quality," [Online]. Available: https://asq.org. [Accessed March 2019].

[15] S. M. Covey, THE SPEED OF TRUST, Simon & Schuster, Inc., 2016.

[16] A. J. Smith, "Society for Human Resource Management (SHRM)," 18 May 2018. [Online]. Available: https://www.shrm.org/resourcesandtools/legal-and-compliance/employment-law/pages/more-employers-ditch-performance-appraisals.aspx. [Accessed April 2019].

[17] R. Bohn, "Stop Fighting Fires," *Havard Business Review,* JULY–AUGUST 2000.

Acknowledgment

I'd like to recognize and thank three groups of people who have enabled and supported my journey and the evolution of CIMS.

The first group are the great leaders who have given me the trust and support to make it happen. Jim Sawyer, who became president of Boeing Canada, gave me my first big opportunity, and taught me the power of optimism. Ken Rowe, the owner and CEO of the IMP Group, known to be a tough and astute businessman, was always very supportive.

And finally, Jim Irving, CEO of J.D. Irving, Limited (JDI), has always been truly committed to operational excellence and would often say "let's do it right".

The second group are the consultants and colleagues from whom I have learned so much. Tom Wallace and Bill Sandras respectively provided the approaches to MPRII and JIT Making It Happen. John Black was instrumental in developing Boeing's World-Class Competitive course, which was my first introduction to a world-class management system. And Merv Symes, Vice President Organizational Change at JDI, exposed me to the concepts of leading change and was instrumental in promoting and evolving CIMS across the enterprise to become the Irving Management System.

The third group, and not the least of course, are the people who really embraced continuous improvement and made it happen. This includes the management and employees in the offices and shop floors who, once empowered, did great things which led to impressive performance improvements.

I want however to recognize specific individuals, who I believe were the driving force behind a lot of this.

At Boeing Arnprior, the place where it really started for me: Brian Needham was a godsent who helped remove the roadblocks; Kevin Ryan, production manager, provided exceptional leadership which led his shop to achieve world-class performance levels; Richard Wiens, Arleen Whitmore and Jonathon Scofield three young bright engineers did a lot of the 'grunt' work; Tom Melvin, the IT guy who was more than an IT guy and eventually became president of Arnprior Aerospace, and; Glen Scheunemann, Lee Dubois, Rick Tabar, Bruce Presley, Eddie Murch, Lindon Jump, and Harold Gross were the old guys, at least relative to my age in those days, who brought it across the line. A great team!

At IMP Aerospace: Dave Miller, the General Manager who I succeeded, kept the 'wolves at bay' while I 'shepherd the herd'; Dave Pearson, who we recruited from the UK as director of Operations and eventually became my successor when I left for Irving; Dale Donovan, who was formally with Boeing Winnipeg; Daniel Leblanc, a young and bright industrial engineer who helped automate the KPIs and facilitated many kaizen blitzes.

And at J.D. Irving: Rheal Maillet, the general manager at Kent Homes, and his key players namely Everard Doiron, Louise Anne Arsenault, and Abbe Lanteigne who together led the implementation of CIMS and Lean to win two years in a row the JK Irving award for most improved business, and; Don Dixon and Kevin Jones were great help and support to increase the maturity of our PMO.

Many thanks to all of you.

About the Author

With over 40 years of experience, Charles Cormier is a results-driven professional renowned for his expertise in continuous improvement and ERP solution delivery. Notably, during his tenure at the Boeing Company, he pioneered Lean methodologies, leading the Canadian Operations to earn numerous awards for elevating to world-class standards. Later, at IMP Aerospace in Amherst, Nova Scotia, he led the operations to become a preferred supplier to major aircraft manufacturers. As divisional vice-president at J.D. Irving, Limited (JDI) – a conglomerate company headquartered in Saint John, New Brunswick – Cormier achieved impressive results through Lean implementation coupled with a continuous improvement framework. Transitioning to Executive Leader of the Project Management Office, he oversaw successful IT solution deliveries, including major ERP projects. Now retired from JDI, Cormier lends his wealth of experience as a consultant, guiding organizations on their paths to excellence.

INDEX

5 Why, 35
5S, 12, 21
5S+1, 94
A Problem Well Understood, Is Half Solved, 34
Ability, 130
ABPMP, 104
ADKAR, 74
Affinitize, 48
Affinitize, 80
Agile, 71
Agile Product Development, 73
Andon cord, 92
APQC, 105, 143
Arsenault, Louise Anne, 160
ASQ, 130
Attack the Problem not the Person, 91
Balance Scorecard, 22, 43, 134
Barriers, 49
Benchmarking, 33, 143
Black, John, 14, 159
Boeing, 5
  Arnprior, 5, 160
  Winnipeg, 15
Boeing's Japan study mission, 14
Brainstorm, 47, 80
business operating model, 58
Catchball, 32, 53
Catchball Process, 39
Change Management Methodologie, 75
Change Manager, 77
Check-Ins, 136
CIMO, 151
CIMS Maturity Model, 147
Continuous Improvement Management Office, 151
Cross-functional Management, 28
Cross-Functional Management, 13, 23
Cross-training matrix, 12
Daily Management, 13, 28
Data Governance, 122
Deming, Doctor W. Edwards, 91, 142
Dixon, Don, 161
Doing it right, 70
Doiron, Everard, 160
Donovan, Dale, 160
Dubois, Lee, 160
Einstein, Albert, 34
Environment, 131
ERP, 23
Fire Fighting, 142
Five Whys, 91
Framework, 29
Gantt Chart, 80
Gemba Walks, 32, 135
Getting it done, 69
Gissing, Bruce, 14, 143
Golden Thread, 53
Gross, Harold, 160
Hemmen, Paul, 8
Hiatt, Jeff, 74
Hoshin Kanri, 38
Hoshin Planning, 53
IASSC, 130
IBP, 58
IBP zones, 61
Identifying Solutions, 51
IMP Group, 16, 159
Initiative Management, 23
Integrated Business Planning, 58
Irving Management System, 23
Irving, Jim, 22, 159
J.D. Irving, 21
J.K. Irving Outstanding Achievement Award, 22

JDI, 21
JIT, 21
Jones, Kevin, 161
Jump, Lindon, 160
Just-in-Time, 10
Just-in-Time: Making it Happen, 11
Kaizen Blitz, 21, 118, 148
Kanbans, 11, 12
Kent Homes, 22
Key Performance Indicator, 44, 109
Kotter, John, 73
KPI, 44, 109
Lanteigne, Abbe, 160
Leading Change, 74
Lean, 10, 30, 70, 114, 151
Lean Six Sigma, 71
Learning Retention, 119
Leblanc, Daniel, 160
Maillet, Rheal, 23, 160
Make It Visual, 88
Making it Happen, 141
Making it stick, 73
Management by Objective, 38
Management by Policy, 13
Management by Walking Around, 135
Maslow's Hierarchy, 128
Maturity Model, 144
MBWA, 135
Melvin, Tom, 160
Miller, Dave, 20, 160
Mission and core values, 43
Motivation, 128
MRPII, 5
MRPII Making it Happen, 7
Murch, Eddie, 160
Needham, Brian, 8, 160
OLAT, 11
Oliver Wight, 7, 8, 11
One-less-at-a-time, 11
Openness, 131
Operating policies, 102
Opportunity Sheet, 90
Pareto Chart, 112
Participative leadership, 31, 129
PDCA, 89
Pearson, Dave, 160
Performance Equation, 128
Performance Management, 29, 127
Plan Management, 29, 37
Plan-Do-Check-Act, 27, 89
PMBOK, 69
PMO, 24
Policy Deployment, 38
Policy Management, 28
Presley, Bruce, 160
PRINCE2, 69
Principles, 31
What Gets Measured, Gets Done, 33
Prioritization of Solutions, 52
Procedures, 102
Process Classification Framework, 102
Process Management, 29, 101
Process Measures, 110
Process Mining, 117
Process Ownership, 106
Progress Management, 29, 87, 136
Progress Meetings, 89
Project Charter, 78
Project governance, 76
Project Management, 29, 67
Frameworks and Methodologies, 68
Project Management Office, 24
Project Manager, 77
Project Plan, 79
Project Sponsor, 77
Project Stage Gates, 83
Project Structure, 76
Prosci, 73
Proven Path, 7, 12
Rapid Improvement Workshop, 12
Respect, 131

Rowe, Ken, 159
Rules of engagement, 81
Ryan, Kevin, 160
Sales and Operation Planning, 58
Sandras, Bill, 11, 159
Sawyer, Jim, 6, 15, 159
Scheunemann, Glen, 160
Scofield, Jonathon, 160
Significant Emotion Events, 143
Six Sigma, 22, 70, 114
Skills Matrix, 137
SMART, 33
SME, 78
Sponsoring Body, 76
Sponsorship coalition, 77
Standardize Work, 93
Steering Committee, 76
STOP proposal, 153
Stop the Line, 92
Strategic Planning Workshop, 40
Strategy Management, 23
Strategy Map, 46
Swimlane, 117
SWOT analysis, 44
Symes, Merv, 23, 159
System Development Life Cycle, 71
Tabar, Rick, 160
Teamwork, 131
Town Hall Meetings, 133
Toyota, 10, 30
TROT, 131
True North, 30
Trust, 32, 131
Value-stream mapping, 115
Virtual Teams, 98
Visibility Board, 12, 88
Vision Statement, 45
Visual Controls, 12
Visual Workplace, 95
Wagile, 73
Wallace, Thomas F., 7, 159
Waste, 115
Waterfall, 71
Water-Scrum-Fall, 73
Whitmore, Arleen, 160
Wiens, Richard, 160
Work Instructions, 94, 102
World Class, 13, 28
World Class Management Systems, 27
World Class Manufacturing, 10
X-matrix, 54

Made in the USA
Monee, IL
16 November 2024

b424476b-5bac-41e4-abd0-0a96cabe7f84R01